STAYING young

STAYING

THOMAS HAGER & LAUREN KESSLER

Facts On File Publications
New York, New York • Oxford, England

To Dorothy Falk, who knows how to live,

and

to Jackson Kessler Hager, who is just learning

STAYING YOUNG

Copyright © 1987 by Tom Hager and Lauren Kessler

Library of Congress Cataloging-in-Publication Data

Hager, Tom.
  Staying young.

  Includes index.
  1. Longevity. 2. Health. 3. Aging. I. Kessler,
Lauren. II. Title.
RA776.75.H33   1987   612'.68   87-5317
ISBN 0-8160-1303-9

Interior text designed by: Ron Monteleone

Composition by Facts On File/Maxwell Photographics

Printed in the United States of America

10 9 8 7 6 5 4 3 2 1

Contents

Preface

A few years ago, one of us went in for a routine physical exam. "You're in great shape," said the doctor, "but wait until you turn 30." The physician, in his mid-40s, seemed to savor the thought. "You'll start slowing down. You'll start going to pot."

Later, we laughed about it.

Then, one by one, we turned 30.

All of a sudden, our metabolisms seemed to screech to a halt. We didn't eat any more than usual, but the scales began tipping in the wrong direction. We discovered our first gray hairs. We peered into the mirror and saw the beginnings of crow's-feet. Our dentist started talking about gum disease. What was happening to us?

We wanted to know. We wanted to know if there were things we could be doing—or not doing—*now* that would help us stay healthy, active and youthful-looking. We wanted to understand the aging process before it conquered us. That's when we first started planning this book.

Since then, we've read dozens of books, reviewed hundreds of scientific studies and questioned scores of experts. We learned a great deal about the aging process—not the least of which was how little researchers know about how and why we age—and what can be done to impede its progress.

One reason so little is known is that the field is so new. Human beings have only recently begun living long enough to care about the aging process. In ancient Greece, the average life span was 22 years. In 1900, it reached 47 years. Today it's 73. Until well into the 20th century, potentially fatal epidemic diseases raged through entire populations. At the turn of the century, one in 16 Americans were 60 or older. Today, it's one in six. When we babyboomers reach retirement age, it will be one in four. Because of these dramatically increasing numbers, the study of aging is just now coming into its own as a field of active scientific inquiry.

Another reason researchers know so little about aging is that the process itself is difficult to study. First, it takes a long time. To accurately study the effects of aging, scientists have to follow the same group of people for decades, patiently waiting for changes to happen. Simply comparing a group of today's young people to a group of today's old people won't work. The older people have grown up with different nutritional and environmental influences that affect the way they've aged. So scientists construct decades-long studies, sit back and wait. The results are just now starting to come in on the studies started in the 50s and 60s.

Second, people don't age in a vacuum. While they're growing older, they may also be smoking, drinking, eating high-fat diets, or suffering from too much stress and too little exercise. How can researchers distinguish between "normal aging" and the long-term effects of lifestyle and environment? They're just beginning to answer this question, and that's what makes aging research one of today's most exciting areas of scientific inquiry.

The latest news from the scientific community is quite encouraging—inactivity and bad habits seem to account for much of what has been considered "normal aging." It's these new findings we report on in the chapters that follow. To us, the message is clear: We *can* do things now, in our 20s, 30s, and 40s, to help us stay healthier and fitter than any previous generation in history.

We are indebted to a number of experts who generously agreed to review portions of this manuscript: Kent Christoferson, M.D., ophthalmology; Cynthia Dreyer, M.D., dermatology; Loyal Ediger, Ph.D., audiology; Gary Glasser, M.D., internal and geriatric medicine; Robert Hackman, Ph.D., nutritional science; Donald Hager, D.D.S., dentistry; John Mundall, M.D., neurology; Byron Musa, M.D., internal medicine and endocrinology; Richard Roberts, Ph.D., muscle physiology; Daniel Robinhold, M.D., cardiology; Cody Wasner, M.D., rheumatology. Their comments and suggestions were invaluable. Any mistakes, of course, are our own.

—L.K. and T.H.
Eugene, Oregon

Part I
THE EVER-CHANGING BODY

1

Aging Well

We don't want to age.

Or rather, we want the knowledge and confidence of age without the gray hair, wrinkles and clogged arteries. Can we have it both ways? We're about to find out.

The past decade has seen an unprecedented explosion in health consciousness. More of us are exercising, eating carefully, watching our weight and keeping in shape than ever before. This new emphasis on fitness is beginning to change the way we think about aging.

At the same time, medical science is rapidly dispelling myths about aging. Responding to the needs of this country's fastest growing population segment—men and women of retirement age—physicians, scientists and government researchers are putting more emphasis on studying the aging process. They are learning that we can stay healthy and fit much longer than anyone ever imagined.

OUR BIOLOGICAL CLOCKS

Birthdates are often a poor indication of age. Human bodies keep their own time, aging at sometimes vastly different rates. What sets the pace of this internal clock? Heredity plays a part. Baldness, for example, is passed down from grandfather to grandson. The speed at which we go gray or lose the youthful elasticity of our skin may also be, in part, a matter of genetics. Heredity may be a factor in certain kinds of age-related hearing loss, arthritis, osteoporosis and heart disease. To age slowly, we should choose our parents well.

But our futures are determined by more than a roll of the DNA dice. The lifestyles we chose and the habits we form greatly influence the speed of our biological clocks. Unprotected sunbathing, for example, is one of the surest, fastest routes to old-looking skin and brittle, lifeless hair. Stress can age us inside and out, contributing to both the serious business of heart attacks and the frivolous concern of graying hair. A typical American high-fat diet can set us up for middle-age spread as it invisibly wreaks havoc on our heart and blood vessels and increases our risk of cancer. Lack of exercise weakens our muscles—including the most important one, the heart—and contributes to problems ranging from obesity to joint disorders. Smoking, best known for its horrific effects on the lungs, also contributes to hardening of the arteries and wrinkling of facial skin. In short, *what we do makes a difference.*

WHAT AGING MEANS

In some societies, older people are integrated into the life of the country, sought after for their knowledge and respected for their experience. But in the United States, the elderly are shut away in retirement ghettos, ignored by politicians and barely tolerated by their own families. It's as if we think aging might be contagious.

Our stereotypes of what it means to grow old tell the story. Aging, we think, is an unrelenting pile-up of aches, pains and indignities. Skin sags, joints creak, arteries clog, backs hunch. And as the complaints mount, so do the medicine bottles on the nightstand. Since most of us know and interact with few *real* older people—they are, after all, effectively hidden from view—we learn about aging from the media. And what we learn is that older women garden and older men golf. Older women bake cookies and older men have heart attacks. Either incontinent or constipated, older people are fragile, sickly and dependent. With images like these, it's no wonder we've come to fear the aging process and expect the worst.

Some expect the worst but see modern science—or at least, cosmetic technology—as the saviors of lost youth. Yes, aging does mean a host of unpalatable changes, but can't the salons, spas and surgeons "fix" all that? Faces can be lifted, tummies tucked, fat suctioned and skin sanded smooth. Exotic creams can erase wrinkles. Expensive machines can tone muscles. Quadruple bypasses can rejuvenate hearts. Aging may mean falling apart, but we can buy our way back to youth and health.

In fact, aging is not an unrelenting descent into decrepitude nor an unsightly disease that can be cured by throwing money at it. It is a natural, life-long process that does not have to mean the quick end to our good health or our good looks. There is such a thing as "aging well," growing into the middle decades and beyond with our minds and bodies intact.

That may sound obvious, but it represents a recent and dramatic shift in how medical researchers view the aging process. Not long ago, they looked at aging as a series of chronic diseases. The body wore itself out just by living, they thought. Now researchers believe the body ages not from overuse but from *disuse*. "The body," writes Stanford researcher James F. Fries in the *New England Journal of Medicine*, "is now felt to rust out rather than wear out." We can do something about disuse, and that means a great deal of the aging process is within our control.

STARTING EARLY

A taste bud gives us two weeks of service before it dies. A red blood cell circulates for four months before it's replaced. A strand of hair lasts five years before it's shed. We may think of aging as something reserved for the end of our lives, but in fact, our bodies are constantly in the process of aging, dying and being reborn.

Our hearing, for example, was most acute when we were newborn and has been fading imperceptibly ever since. The gland that controls our immune system has been shrinking since puberty. By 20, cholesterol has already started building up in our arteries, and our brain has stopped growing. Since mid-20s, our eyes have been changing, and our bones may have been losing density.

Obviously, none of us are too young to concern ourselves with aging well. And, the earlier we concern ourselves, the better our chances of lessening or postponing many of the effects of aging. For not all the changes we think of as inevitable actually are. Most digestive problems are not a consequence of aging. Neither is hardening of the arteries, loss of muscle tone or middle-age spread. We don't automatically lose flexibility, endurance and stamina because we grow older. Our memory doesn't automatically worsen; our sex drive doesn't automatically fade.

In fact, many of the changes we think of as the result of growing older are actually the cumulative effects of bad habits and late 20th century living. Researchers say inactivity accounts for about half of our functional decline between ages 30 and 70. Scientists say the typical American high-fat, low-fiber diet is a major cause of heart disease and many digestive disorders. On the other hand, studies show that relaxation techniques can help keep blood pressure down. Various vitamins and minerals can contribute to everything from a strong immune system to a healthy set of teeth. Regular, vigorous exercise can keep our weight down, muscles toned and heart young.

We *can* age well. The key is understanding how we age, and what we can do now to slow the process.

2
Why We Age

Aging is the ultimate insult. Just when we reach the peak of our physical powers, in our late 20s to early 30s, we start falling apart. Our bodies begin weakening, withering, wrinkling, until—if nothing else gets us first—we die of old age.

It's no wonder humans throughout history have raged and fought against growing old. All of recorded history is studded with amazing stories, suspect advice and bizarre treatments for halting the march of time. Youth-seekers have tried everything from inhaling virgin's breath (see sidebar) to imbibing alchemical potions made with powdered gold. Physicians hoping to slow time have implanted patients with monkey testicles and injected them with sheep hormones. It seems humans have always sought ways to extend life, to beat nature, to stay young forever.

THE BREATH OF VIRGINS

Some of the many "cures" for old age developed through the centuries fall into the category of wishful thinking. An example from an 18th-century physician, Cohausen: "In five beds in a small room let there lie five virgins under the age of thirteen, and of wholesome constitution; then in the spring of the year, about the beginning of the month of May, let there be a hole pierced through the wall of the chamber..."

Through the hole, wrote the good doctor, insert the long neck of a flask used for distilling. The warm breath of the young girls would then flow into the flask and condense into "a clear water, which is a tincture of admirable efficacy...an *elixir vitae.*" Just a few drops, wrote Cohausen, could make the old young again, and keep one "remote from the shadow of death." By way of a testimonial, he told of an aged Consul of Venice who surrounded himself with young girls. This venerable old goat was never sick, according to Cohausen; his hair turned from white to black at age 100, he cut two new teeth at 113 and didn't die until the year 1702, at the ripe age of 115.

But, according to modern medical science, no one's done it—yet. Normal aging is still with us, as much a part of life as birth and death, a process basically unchanged since humans evolved a million years ago.

Don't be misled by statistics that say we're now living longer than ever before. They refer to the *average* age at death of a total population. Groups with a high infant mortality rate, for instance, have low average lifespans—despite the fact that a few members may live to very old ages. The *maximum* human life span has not gone up one day since prehistoric times. The maximum figure seems to be a biologically set limit on everyone's life, a fixed number of years beyond which no one can live.

AVERAGE VS. MAXIMUM LIFE SPAN

All the advances of science and technology, all the phalanxes of physicians and masses of medical machinery we have today haven't extended the *maximum* age to which a person can live by even a single day. Our maximum life span—the longest an individual can possibly live, barring accidents or diseases—hovers at about 120 years. There's no good evidence that anyone, anywhere, at any time has ever lived longer.

Yes, there are reports of longer-lived peoples inhabiting various hard-to-reach areas around the world—Shangri-las in the Caucasus Mountains, the Andes, the Himalayas — but scientific studies invariably find that the reports are either untrue or unverifiable. According to one study, the longest-lived human with complete credentials was Fanny Thomas, who attributed her longevity to eating applesauce three times a day and never marrying, so that "I never had a man to bother me." Fanny died in 1980 in California at the age of 113 years, 215 days.

Average lifespans have been going up. Citizens of ancient Rome could expect to live only about 22 years. In the U.S. in 1900, the average life span had increased to nearly 50 years. Now, in most industrialized Western countries, the average life span is about 74 years. These increases are due to lower infant mortality and the virtual elimination of many deadly diseases.

But we're reaching the end of the benefits to be gained by beating diseases. Curing all forms of cancer, for instance, would boost the average life span in the United States by only about two years. Ridding our planet of every human disease, all wars and accidents would raise the average life span only into the low 90s—still far short of immortality.

THE BIOLOGICAL SYMPHONY

Despite the age-old concern with growing older, *we still don't know why we age*. Modern science has recently taken up the search for the roots of aging, armed with the ability to peer inside cells and tear apart biological systems molecule by molecule.

But these scientific explorers are hindered by a basic problem: aging is intimately tied to some of science's most puzzling mysteries. Right now, we understand more about the physical laws that bind a single atom together than we do about the biological processes that make our aging bodies fall apart.

Blame our biological intricacy. We are dauntingly complex organisms, each a walking world made up of billions of cells—more cells in each person than there are people on the earth. We are whole ecosystems bound in skin, a delicate balance of interwoven structures.

This biological symphony is conducted by DNA, the genetic material that carries the instructions that make us what we are. DNA controls the mysterious process by which a single fertilized egg cell in a woman's womb flawlessly multiplies into the millions of specialized cells that make up a baby. How this process, called cellular differentiation, is controlled is one of the biggest puzzles facing biologists today.

After a baby is born, the body's changes continue, somehow transforming an eight-pound baby into an over-100-pound adult. Cellular differentiation lies at the heart of aging research, for without understanding how it occurs, it may be impossible to finally understand why the billions of cells in an older adult eventually fail—why we age.

But that hasn't stopped scientists from theorizing about the causes of aging. A number of competing theories are now being tossed around in scientific journals, one or a combination of which may someday prove to be the right answer. They fall generally into two groups.

PROGRAMMED DESTRUCTION

The first group of theories contends that we are somehow programmed to age and die just as we're programmed to grow from child to adult.

THE LIMITS OF LIFE

Organism	Maximum Lifespan (yr.)
Bristlecone Pine	6,000 +
Coast Redwood	2,500 +
Marion's Tortoise	152 +
Man	120
Freshwater Mussel	100
Sea Anemone	90
Elephant	70
Eagle Owl	68
Horse	62

Organism	Maximum Lifespan (yr.)
Giant Salamander	52 +
Chimpanzee	45
Domestic Dog	34
Domestic Cat	28
Mouse	3.5

It's as though each plant and animal is fitted with a biological clock that starts ticking at birth, gradually running down and stopping after a given number of years. For some creatures the clock runs down quickly, for others it takes centuries, but the outcome is the same: When the clock quits ticking, so do we.

The program theory sees aging as an ordered part of human development. Part of the evidence comes from studies of human fetal development. As a fetus grows in the womb, its shape changes drastically. At one point in development, the human fetus has webbed toes and fingers. The cells that form the webbing eventually die and are sloughed off. They are somehow programmed to die—must die if a normal baby is to be born. Some researchers believe that if these cells are programmed to die, there may be similar programs directing large numbers of cells in an aged person to self-destruct. Aging, dying cells, these scientists say, then lead to aging, dying organs—resulting in aging, dying people.

More direct evidence for an aging program in cells has come from laboratory experiments like those carried out by Leonard Hayflick, a researcher now at the University of Florida. Hayflick is an expert in the delicate scientific technique called tissue culture. This painstaking craft involves separating living cells from the body and convincing them to grow in plastic flasks filled with warm nutrient broth. Tissue culture is an important way of studying the effects of chemicals and drugs—and aging—on individual cells.

But a vexing problem faces everyone who works with normal cells in tissue culture: At first the cells grow and divide healthily in their plastic home, but after a certain number of generations, the cells all die. Hayflick experimented with many types of animal cells, and from different parts of the body, but no matter where the cells came from, they would divide in culture only a set number of times. Then, as though their internal clock was nearing its last few ticks, the cells would show signs of aging and die. Hayflick found that cells from older animals would die after fewer generations than cells from younger animals, and that cells from short-lived animal types—like mice—died out sooner than cells from longer-lived species—like humans. No matter how ideal the tissue culture growth conditions, no amount of cajoling could push the cells beyond their preset time limit. Each individual cell seemed to have its own program that told it how many times it could divide before dying—a phenomenon now known as the Hayflick limit.

DNA is the most likely site for this self-destruct program. This would help explain the fact that long-lived parents tend to have long-lived children, since the program would be passed from generation to generation. Our maximum lifespan limit also fits neatly with this theory: After 120 years, our cells are simply programmed to stop regenerating and expire. And the program theory is hard to disprove because ultimately the proof depends on things we still know little about—such as how DNA controls our growth and development.

But why would a species develop an aging program, a built-in guarantee of death? The scientists have an answer for this, too: sex. In addition to its other benefits, sex provides a way for different individuals to mix their genes, producing offspring with a new genetic makeup. The result is genetic diversity, vital for a species trying to survive in a changing environment.

But the sex-for-diversity system comes with a built-in drawback. This constant mixing of genes requires the constant creation of new individuals—and they all need room and food. In evolutionary terms, the old have to make room for the young. What better way to do it than to make sure—through a genetic program for aging—that the older generation dies?

THE ATTACK

Critics of the program theory aren't convinced. Some say cells die when they're cultured not because of an aging program but because science hasn't yet figured out the ideal conditions for growing cells in culture. When we do, they say, the cells will live well beyond what one researcher calls "the notorious Hayflick limit." More importantly, they point out, not all cells have a Hayflick limit. While *normal* body cells will stop growing in culture after a certain number of generations, *cancer* cells do not. Cancer cells and cells in precancerous states have been grown in lab bottles for decades without losing any vigor. Somehow these cell lines have bypassed the Hayflick limit; they are immortal. If some cells aren't programmed to age, the critics say, maybe none are.

Instead, these researchers theorize that either our environment or our own metabolism slowly ages us like a piece of hard-run rusting machinery. Although the attacks may come from a number of different places, they have, according to most theories, a single target: DNA. When the genetic material of the cell is attacked and injured, the cell can't function normally.

Free Radicals

Nasty bits of molecular debris called free radicals may be DNA's greatest enemy. These unstable troublemakers are fragments of molecules that have been smashed apart during chemical reactions. Free radicals seek to reunite with something—anything in the cell—to become whole again. Unfortunately, many of the things they react with are the wrong things. Free radicals damage cell membranes and structural proteins. More importantly, they can mangle DNA.

And we make them ourselves when we turn oxygen into energy, a process that must go on if life is to continue. Since they're an unavoidable menace, our bodies have devised ways of dealing with them. Each cell contains several enzymes to sop up or deactivate free radicals. In addition, every cell has a repair system to correct the DNA damage created by free radicals.

With all this protection, why are free radicals considered a cause of aging? Because sometimes the damage they inflict on DNA is so great that repair systems are unable to deal with it. Theorists say that the DNA damage may accumulate, triggering the aging of cells—and thus of the body.

Error Buildup

There are other ways of damaging DNA. Each time a cell divides, a new copy of the DNA must be made. During this replication process it is possible, some researchers say, for the cell's replication machinery to make mistakes; the new copy might not be perfect. Generation after generation, these mistakes could build up, causing the changes we see as aging and eventually killing the cell.

Molecular Garbage

Another postulated attack-from-within might come from the piling up of molecular garbage. Some scientists argue that certain molecules tend to avoid cellular housecleaning, accumulating over time and eventually gumming up normal cellular functioning. A prime candidate is lipofuscin, a fatty brown pigment that can collect in some tissues to the point where it may cause the changes we call aging. Other suspects include glucose, a common sugar that can damage proteins and bind molecules together into a tangled mess, and amyloid, a jumble of several proteins that accumulates with age.

Immune Breakdown

Others theorize that aging is due to the body attacking itself. The culprit here is the immune system—the intricate interplay of white blood cells and antibodies that helps us fight off germs, viruses and other foreign invaders. With age, the immune system loses some of its ability to recognize harmful substances and, according to some researchers, it may even start attacking the body itself, destroying healthy cells and leading to a breakdown in normal functioning. This theory, of course, begs the question of why the immune system itself ages.

A CURE FOR AGING?

Each of these major theories has its variations and subtheories, each with its own vocal group of proponents. The interest in this area indicates both how hard scientists are searching for the causes of aging, and how much remains to be done.

But not knowing why we age hasn't stopped many people—respected scientists among them—from putting forth pet ideas on ways to slow or stop the aging process. Roy Walford, a noted UCLA gerontologist and major architect of the immune theory of aging, believes that undernutrition—a diet that provides for all our metabolic needs, but is very low in calories—can extend the maximum lifespan of humans. Walford admits, however, that the scientific studies supporting his theory have been done only with rats, mice or other animals—not with humans. Nobody knows at this point how undernutrition affects any of the possible causes of aging listed above.

Other gurus of aging have their own dietary plans, many centering on the consumption of massive doses of vitamins, minerals and a class of free-radical-fighting chemicals called antioxidants. And diet isn't the only path to extended longevity, according to various doctors, believers and quacks. Many people travel to Europe or Mexico for exotic "rejuvenation" therapies involving injections of cells from fetal animals, or treatment with novocaine-like drugs. Despite enthusiastic testimonials from believers, the bottom line with all these therapies is that none has been *proven* to work by the rigorous testing required by medical science.

Charlatans flourish because so little is known about aging, and so many want to stay young. But no one has yet discovered the fountain of youth. All we can do now is to try to understand what there is to know about our aging bodies—and to follow the youth-maintaining advice given by physicians and researchers in the following chapters.

Part II
LOOKING GOOD

3

Hair

We twirl, curl, cut and pluck it. We shave, brush, tint and wax it. We wash it, brush it, braid and pomade it. We spend more than $2 billion a year pampering it and have more of it per square inch than a chimpanzee. When it begins to turn gray, we panic. When it begins to recede, we have mid-life crises.

Hair. Both fine and coarse, it covers our bodies, leaving bare only a few, odd patches. To scientists it's superficial shafts of dead protein emerging from follicles deep within the skin. Its primary function, say the scientists, is protection: Body hair evolved from thick, insulating fur. Hair guards the scalp from the sun's rays; the eyebrows and eyelashes protect the eyes from foreign particles.

But to us it's decoration, ornamentation and self-expression. We know hair's primary function is fashion. That's why we're devastated when our hair shows the signs of aging.

And age it does, although in somewhat different ways and at slightly different rates, depending on who we are and how we take care of ourselves. Some of the changes we associate with aging—brittle or lifeless hair, a certain kind of baldness—are actually the result of our own neglect or abuse and can be prevented. But most of the changes are inevitable: A man genetically programmed to go bald will go bald. All of us go gray sooner or later.

Still, there's no good medical reason to worry about these changes. Unlike an aging back or an aging heart, aging hair has no effect whatsoever on our health. And, in the case of hair, the inevitable is not necessarily the inescapable. For those who don't find a graying or balding head attractive, there are a growing number of alternatives.

KNOW YOUR HAIR

A single hair begins as a clump of cells at the base of a tiny bulb (follicle) buried in the skin's inner layer. As new cells grow, the older ones die, harden and are pushed upward until they break the surface of the skin. This visible hair shaft is more than 95 percent keratin (a particular kind of protein) and 100 percent dead. That's important to remember when you evaluate hair products claiming to "feed" and "nourish" the hair shaft. You can't feed dead tissue.

The shaft is made of three layers. The inner layer of cells gives hair its strength. The middle layer, with its granules of pigment, gives hair its color. The outer layer, known as the cuticle, protects the underlying layers with an armor of overlapping scale-like cells arranged like the shingles on a roof. The entire hair shaft is covered with a protective acid (4.5 to 5.5 pH) mantle made up of a thin film of oils, fatty acids and salts.

Why know all this? Because alkaline (above 7 pH) hair products—that includes most shampoos and all soaps, perm solutions and hair colorings—disrupt the hair's protective acid mantle and swell the cuticle layer. The shingled cells open up rather than lie flat, causing split ends and making the delicate middle layer vulnerable to the environment. Hair products with the same pH as hair itself, 4.5 to 5.5, are the ones to use.

The average scalp has 110,000 hairs—redheads have the least, blonds the most—which are programmed to grow, rest, shed and regrow in a continuous cycle. At any given moment, about 85 percent of the hairs are growing, while 15 percent are resting or being shed. That means continuous shedding (up to 100 hairs a day) is a natural part of the process of growing a healthy head of hair. Each strand of hair grows three to six inches a year for up to five years. Then it rests for three to four months before it's shed and the follicle begins producing a replacement.

WHAT HAPPENS TO HAIR AS WE AGE?

Beginning in our late 20s to early 30s, we begin to see the signs. By our late 30s or early 40s, they are unmistakable. Our hair is announcing our age. Here's what happens:

- **Hair dries out.** The oil glands that lubricate the hair (and the skin) become increasingly inactive as we age. For oily hair sufferers, that's a blessing—up to a point. But as the trend continues, the hair begins to suffer. Lack of lubrication leaves it brittle, vulnerable to breaking, splitting and further harm from the environment.
- **Hair gets finer.** As we age, the thickness of each hair shaft decreases, as the protein-making machinery of the body slows down. At 40, the hair shaft is 5 percent thinner than it was at 20. According to statistics compiled by the Orentreich Institute for the Advancement of Science—Dr. Norman Orentreich is a pioneer hair researcher—the hairs on the head of a 70-year-old man are as fine as they were when he was a baby. And fine hair, even if one has as much of it as one always did, looks less luxuriant.
- **Hair turns gray.** Actually, there's no such thing as gray hair. What we see as gray is the mix between normally pigmented hair and aging white hair. Technically, there's no such thing as white hair either. What we see as white hair is actually colorless; the way light bounces off it makes it appear white. When we age, pigment production within the hair cells decreases, leaving the shaft colorless. The more colorless ("white") hairs, the "grayer" we look.
- **Hair falls out.** Some shedding is part of the hair's normal growth cycle and not age-related. But as we get older, stress, diet, drugs—and especially hormones—can cause hair to fall out and not be replaced in kind. The American Medical Association estimates that more than a third of all 35-year-old men have noticeable hair loss. At 45, almost half are balding. Thinning is a problem for both sexes. At 20, the average head sports 700 hairs per square centimeter; at 50, it has only 500 in the same area.
- **Hair grows where you don't want it.** In one of nature's little ironies, aging hair grows less where you want it—the scalp—and more where you don't. For men, this may mean increasingly bushy eyebrows and hair sprouting from the nostrils and ears. Some men get hairy backs as they age. Older women may be distressed to discover facial hair.

HOW WE DAMAGE OUR HAIR

It's dry and brittle. It has neither sheen nor body. This unhealthy, old-looking, damaged hair is not a consequence of the normal aging process. Abuse and thoughtlessness are the causes. We physically damage our hair by treating it roughly. We chemically damage our hair by using harsh products. We nutritionally damage our hair by not feeding it from within.

FIVE MYTHS ABOUT HAIR CARE

1. *MYTH*: Brushing your hair 100 strokes a day keeps it shiny and healthy. *FACT*: Excessive brushing actually damages hair. Twenty strokes is more like it. Gently.
2. *MYTH*: Shampooing daily weakens hair and makes it limp. *FACT*: Daily shampooing (with the right product) promotes healthy hair and may be a necessity for those who live amid urban pollutants.
3. *MYTH*: Shampoos or conditioners rich in protein, DNA, RNA, collagen or keratin can feed the hair shaft, making it thicker and healthier. *FACT*: Once it emerges from your scalp, hair is dead tissue. Its structure cannot be permanently improved.
4. *MYTH*: Sun-drying your hair is healthy and natural. *FACT*: It may be be "natural," but the sun is one of your hair's worst enemies. It dries out the hair shaft and leads to split ends.
5. *MYTH*: Split ends are curable. *FACT*: The conditioners claiming to cure split ends merely cement them to the hair shaft temporarily. There is only one real cure: Cut them off.

In our 30s and 40s—genes willing—our hair can be as lustrous and full-bodied as it was in our 20s, if we recognize and mend our abusive ways. Here are the major culprits and how to guard against them:

- **The sun.** Ultraviolet rays are one of the hair's worst enemies, because they cause the hair shaft to dry out and the ends to split. Although ultraviolet light is sometimes prescribed for certain kinds of scalp conditions, sunlight—including sunlamps and tanning beds—robs the hair of its natural moisture, making it look and feel brittle. Avoid this damage by covering your head when you work or play in the sun. During the summer or in hot, dry climates, use especially rich conditioners to remoisturize the hair shaft.

- **Blow driers.** Unnaturally hot air can cause serious hair damage. Regular blasts of scorching air will cause progressive, cumulative damage first to the cuticle, then to the hair's inner layers. The shaft becomes dry, brittle and split. High heat can also scorch the scalp and even kill follicles beneath the skin. The worst of it is, the more "efficient" a blow drier is (the faster it dries your hair), the more damage it can do. The air is hotter and comes out with greater force. Allowing your hair to dry naturally may be inconvenient, but it's the only way to avoid this damage. If you must blow-dry, use a low-wattage appliance, keep it as far from your scalp as you can and don't use it every day.

- **Harsh chemical products.** Most, but not all shampoos, hair-coloring solutions, permanent-wave mixtures and hair straighteners cause chemical damage, because they strip away the hair's protective acid mantle, swell the hair shaft and raise the shingles of the cuticle. Moisture escapes through the raised cuticle, allowing the hair to become dry and brittle. Pay attention to what you or your hairdresser puts on your hair. Choose a shampoo with a pH close to the hair's own 4.5 to 5.5. Follow any treatment using a high pH (alkaline) hair product with a low pH (acidic) rinse or conditioner to close the shingles of the cuticle layer.

- **Overzealous brushing.** Brushing hair too much or too vigorously can cause what's called traction baldness—temporary, self-induced hair loss, the result of physically yanking the hair shaft out of the scalp. Brushing wet hair is one sure way to worsen the problem. The frictional force on wet hair is about five times that on dry hair. Backcombing or "teasing" hair may temporarily add body, but in the long run, it does just the opposite. Each stroke abrades the hair's outer layer, opening the shingled cells, splitting ends and exposing the inner layers to damage and moisture loss. Treat hair gently.

- **Damaging hairstyles.** Braids, cornrows, ponytails and any hairstyle using rubber bands or tightly clamped barrettes put tension on the hair shaft and can lead to traction baldness. If the hair isn't actually pulled from the scalp, it can be stretched and broken. Tight braids crimp and twist the hair, making outer-layer damage inevitable. Avoid these hairstyles. If you must put your hair up, never keep it in one of these styles overnight. Brush very gently after you take it down.

- **Hair spray.** Used by both men and women, especially when short styles are fashionable, hair spray is largely alcohol. That means one of its major effects is to dry out the hair shaft, making it brittle and prone to breaking. It also coats the hair with a sticky film that attracts dust and makes hair look dull. Find a hairstyle that doesn't require spray to keep it looking good.

- **Poor nutrition.** Fad diets or diets low in protein, iron, B vitamins or essential minerals can damage hair from within by robbing the body of the raw materials it needs to create strong, healthy hair. Eat well, remembering that healthy hair is grown, not created in the salon.

FOOD FOR YOUR HAIR

Healthy hair grows from within. No expensive salon treatments or exotic formulas can do as much to keep your hair looking and acting young as a diet rich in these essential nutrients:

Nutrient	Need	Source
Protein	Hair is 98 percent protein.	fish, eggs, meats, cheese
B vitamins	counteract effects of stress; stimulate cell growth and repair	whole grains, eggs, liver, wheat germ
vitamin E	promotes healthy scalp	green vegetables, seeds, nuts, whole grains
vitamin C	repairs follicle injury	citrus fruits, leafy vegetables

Nutrient	Need	Source
Calcium	hair and nail strength	dairy products
Zinc	cell growth, vitamin synthesis	shellfish, red meat, wheat germ

GOING GRAY

Gray hair is the common denominator of human aging, the single, most prevalent sign that we're growing older. Some people notice a scattering of white strands in their 20s; others don't spot a single one until well into their 30s. Some may even sail through their 40s without noticeable graying. But everyone goes gray sooner or later. For most people, white hairs first appear around the temples and gradually move upward toward the crown.

Scientists know *what* happens—as we age, pigment production decreases in the hair shaft's middle layer—but they don't know *why*. There are some clues, however. In lab experiments, black rats fed diets deficient in B vitamins—the vitamins the human body calls upon during times of stress—turned prematurely gray. When B vitamins were added back to their diet, their hair returned to its normal color. Perhaps nutritional imbalance contributes to graying, suggest some researchers. Maybe stress plays a role in the process.

Everyone knows good nutrition is essential to overall health, but some scientists and most naturopathic and chiropractic physicians believe in the power of individual nutrients to slow the aging process—including the graying of hair. Vitamin B supplements, they say, can do this. Other researchers insist that a vitamin B deficiency severe enough to cause premature graying is an extremely rare condition.

Most agree that stress can cause us to go gray before our time. The person who experiences a severe emotional shock and seems to sprout a head of white hairs overnight attests to this. (This can, in fact, happen.) In general, hard-driving fast-trackers who haven't learned how to relax show all the signs of aging—including gray hair—before the rest of us.

While it's possible that our gray hairs are premature and can be blamed on vitamin deficiencies, emotional stress or certain diseases, it's far more likely that they come to us naturally via our genetic heritage. As yet, no one has figured out how to prevent or reverse this process. But the multi-billion-dollar hair products industry has created some temporary alternatives to gray hair.

What can you do when you discover you're going gray? Here are some suggestions:

- **Stay natural.** Gray hair can be strikingly attractive and can add to your authority and presence.
- **Use semipermanent rinses.** Do-it-yourselfers who want to cover up a partially gray head can use a variety of at-home products. Buy a shade of hair rinse slightly lighter than your own, suggest hairdressers. That way the color won't show on pigmented hair but will turn the white strands into highlights. Choosing a color darker than your own produces a flat, harsh, unnatural look. Semipermanent rinses wash out gradually in six to eight shampoos.
- **Get professional highlighting.** This process is ideal for dark-haired people who have less than 40 percent white hair but don't want to look gray at all. A hairdresser applies a variety of highlights in brown, chestnut and dark blond shades. When done skillfully, no gray is evident and no touch-ups are needed between sessions. Highlighting need only be done three or four times a year.
- **Use permanent color.** For mostly gray or unevenly gray hair, permanent hair dye may be the only answer. Dye can completely change the color of your hair, but its most "natural" application is in a shade slightly lighter than your own. Depending on how quickly your hair grows—and your gray roots begin to show—permanent color must be reapplied every four to eight weeks.

BALDNESS AND HAIR LOSS

About one out of eight men experiences noticeable baldness by age 25, estimates the American Medical Association. During the next ten years, three times as many male hairlines can be seen beating a speedy retreat. By age 45, close to half the male population shows obvious signs of so-called pattern baldness. At retirement age, 65 percent of men are at least partially bald.

But baldness isn't limited to men. While no one knows exactly how many women are affected, some dermatologists report that an increasing number of women in their 20s and 30s are losing their hair for stress-related reasons. And it's been known for years that some post-menopausal women suffer significant hair loss.

FIVE MYTHS ABOUT BALDNESS

1. MYTH: Baldness is a sign of lack of virility. FACT: Actually, it's just the opposite: Excessive amounts of the male hormone testosterone cause hair loss.
2. MYTH: Women don't go bald. FACT: Female baldness follows a different pattern and is rarer than male pattern baldness, but it certainly exists. Postmenopausal women are most at risk.
3. MYTH: Frequent shampooing can cause hair loss. FACT: Frequent shampooing may actually help retard male pattern baldness by stimulating blood circulation to hair follicles.
4. MYTH: Shedding means you're going bald. FACT: Shedding up to 100 hairs a day is normal and means that your hair is healthy and growing.
5. MYTH: Scalp massage stimulates hair growth. FACT: Vigorous or frequent scalp massage can actually contribute to hair loss by physically damaging the hair shaft.

Researchers have yet to figure out why people go bald, although they've been pondering the question for hundreds of years. At a 17th-century symposium, poisons in the air were blamed. During the 19th century, American medical students were taught that "brain expansion" due to high-level intellectual activity led to hair loss. Slaves and women, by virtue of their supposedly small brains and insignificant thoughts, were considered immune to baldness. Today's scientists say that 90 percent of all male baldness and some female baldness is genetically programmed—but they don't know the details.

They do know that the unlucky scalps contain hair follicles genetically sensitive to the male hormone testosterone. Women have this hormone too, but their abundant supply of estrogen—at least through their 40s—fights the effects of testosterone, even if their follicles are sensitive. Left undefended, sensitive follicles shrink and begin producing fewer and more fragile hairs, more like those normally grown on the arms than the head.

This genetic program is activated by age. In men, the result generally follows a pattern (hence the term "pattern baldness"): A gradually receding widow's peak in front eventually meets a growing "monk's spot" in back, leaving only a narrow horseshoe of hair around the head. Women tend to lose hair willy-nilly, resulting in sparse overall coverage with no true bald spots.

But ten percent of all men who lose their hair—and virtually all premenopausal women who lose their hair—aren't genetically programmed to go bald. Why do they?

- **Stress.** Tension or stress can cause a large number of hair follicles to go into a resting stage and then shed. The resulting patchy baldness may be caused by the stressed-out body mistakenly producing antibodies which attack part of the hair follicle. Stress may also stimulate the adrenal glands to produce more hair-hostile male hormones.
- **Nutritional deficiencies.** Extended fasts and crash diets starve the system of protein, causing the body to break down its own tissue in search of this vital nutrient. The body considers hair, which is almost all protein, a primary source. Lack of dietary protein can also send the hair into a resting phase which ends in massive shedding. Deficiencies in either iron or zinc are known to cause hair loss. At the other extreme, vitamin enthusiasts may bring on baldness by unintentionally overdosing on vitamin A.
- **Drugs or radiation.** Almost any drug, if taken in high enough doses for a long time, can cause heavy hair loss—even aspirin. Cancer drugs are the worst offenders. Anticoagulants, some antidepressants and beta blockers (used to treat high blood pressure) may also cause appreciable hair loss. Birth control pills—*after* you stop taking them—can cause excessive shedding as the body's estrogen levels return to normal. X-rays are another known culprit.
- **Illness or surgery.** High fevers and physical trauma both disrupt the hair's normal growth cycle, causing premature resting and shedding. Hair loss—sometimes massive—usually occurs two or three months after the shock.

- **Hair abuse.** Lengthy, vigorous brushing, tight rubber bands and tautly pulled hairstyles all can yank hairs from the head, causing noticeable thinness around the temples.
- **Pregnancy.** A few months after giving birth, while the body is in the midst of readjusting its hormonal balance, some women may lose quite a lot of hair. Pregnancy-induced inflated estrogen levels keep the hair in a longer growing phase than normal. When the hormone decreases, all the hair that should have shed but didn't, does.

Is there a cure for baldness? The afflicted have been asking that question—and hotly pursuing the latest treatment—since an ancient Egyptian queen suggested using a salve of dates and dog's toes. Actually, the answer is quite simple: If the baldness is caused by one of the temporary conditions mentioned above, there is a cure: time. Hair almost always grows back normally after the follicles recuperate from whatever temporary shock they received. But if you are genetically programmed to go bald, as 90 percent of men who go bald are, there is only one known cure: castration. Most would choose baldness. For women genetically programmed to lose hair, estrogen therapy sometimes works, but the trade-offs include increased risk of certain cancers.

Contrary to what vitamin peddlers assert, there is no reputable evidence showing that megadoses of various substances—vitamin E, zinc, inositol and PABA are among those touted—cure baldness, unless the baldness is a direct (temporary) result of a massive nutritional deficiency. Over-the-counter drugs promising to grow hair on balding heads do not work. In fact, the FDA banned them in 1985, calling the whole industry "an area of considerable consumer fraud." Two other cosmetic "cures" for baldness, hair weaving and hair implants, have gotten deservedly bad press. Hair weaving, which involves anchoring wig hair to existing scalp hair, actually encourages further hair loss by placing added tension on existing hair. The implant technique, which surgically attaches synthetic hair to the scalp, frequently results in infection, abscesses and major hair loss.

Doesn't modern science have any good news for the genetically programmed bald person who wants a full head of hair? Of course it does:

- **Individually styled and fitted hairpieces and wigs.** If you have the money, there's no reason to look like Howard Cosell. Hairpiece technology is so sophisticated that it really is possible for only your hairdresser to know for sure.

- **Hair transplants.** Developed in 1950s, this technique involves the transplanting of "plugs," each consisting of 12-15 intact hairs and follicles, from the back of the head to the bald spots. But the process is tedious and costly, and not everyone has enough hair to provide sufficient plugs. The newest solution is hair transplantation combined with scalp-reduction surgery.
- **Minoxidil.** A drug used to treat high blood pressure, Minoxidil appears to have an unusual side effect: It grows hair. More than 20 U.S. researchers are currently studying the drug's effect on both male pattern baldness and a disease causing patchy baldness (*alopecia areata*). Rubbed into the scalp, the drug is winning rave reviews in the experimental stage, but the FDA has yet to approve it. One Northwestern University researcher reported regrowth on 50 percent of bald heads within three months.

THE INCREDIBLE SHRINKING BALD SPOT

Doctors can now shrink a bald spot the size of a palm to the width of a finger with a cosmetic surgery technique akin to a face lift. The newly narrowed bald spot can then be reforested with transplanted hair plugs.

A plastic surgeon or dermatologist makes a cut in the crown, then tugs the scalp upward, pulling the hair-covered side areas toward the center bald spot. The excess skin is cut away, and the scalp is stitched together. Performed under local anesthetic, the 60-minute procedure can be repeated to further reduce the size of a bald spot. The cost each time: $1,200.

But not all scalps take to the procedure. Doctors say that in a quarter of the cases, the scalp is too tight to be stretched. But for those who are eligible, scalp-reduction surgery followed by hair-plug transplants can mean the end to a shiny pate.

UNWANTED HAIR

Some people are just genetically hairier than others. Whites are hairier than blacks, who are in turn hairier than Orientals. Southern Europeans are hairier than Northern Europeans. But for others, hormones, not genes, are to blame. Ironically, the same male hormone that attacks the thick hair on scalps causes luxuriant hair growth where it isn't wanted: ears, nose, eyebrows and backs for men; face and body for women. Happily, both men and women generally sail through their 30s and 40s without this hormonally induced growth. But when women's estrogen levels drop after menopause or when age or genetic predisposition make men more sensitive to their own male hormones, the problems begin.

There are ways to get rid of unwanted hair. Drugs that lower the concentration of male hormones in the body or interfere with the body's ability to respond to them—birth control pills and cortisone drugs are examples—can help. But these drugs may have side effects even more unwelcome than the hair itself. Unless the problem is of major proportions, doctors recommend the more conventional hair removal methods: cutting, shaving, tweezing, waxing or using depilatories. Only electrolysis, the costly, time-consuming and painful killing of follicles by electrical current, will permanently remove unwanted hair.

4

The Skin

We tingle, twitch, shiver, sweat, blush and blister. We itch and smart, prickle and quiver, feeling pain and pleasure as we react to the world around us. What enables us to do all this is the finely layered tissue that sheathes the bone and muscle—the resilient bag, paper thin, that holds us together: the skin.

At two square yards, it is the body's largest organ—and its most contradictory. It both separates us from our environment and allows us to experience it. It defines us, isolates us, hems us in; but at the same time it gives us the means to go beyond ourselves, to interact with wind, water and each other. Our ally against everything from grime to germs, it betrays our moods, our habits—and our age. Wrinkled, dry, lined and sagging skin is one of the first, most noticeable and most unwelcome signs of aging. But is is, at the same time, one of the least physically damaging changes that will happen to us as we age. Wrinkles and lines may hurt us psychologically, but they do relatively little to interfere with the vital functions of the skin or the survival of our bodies. Although certain cell and tissue changes make the skin somewhat less efficient at what it does, it continues to do its job more than adequately for as long as we need it.

Yet the longer we live, the more our faces announce the fact. Researchers know *what* happens when skin ages, but they've yet to discover *why*.

SKIN FROM THE OUTSIDE IN

The skin's outer layer, the epidermis, is the body's first protection against the hostile outside world. Organized into four or five tiers of cells (palms and soles are the thickest), the epidermis contains melanin, a dark pigment that colors our skin. Every day millions of new skin cells are created in the bottommost tier of the epidermis. As the cells multiply, they push up toward the surface, becoming part of successive layers until they reach the top. There they die and are continuously shed and replaced. The skin we see, this top tier of the epidermis—composed only of dead cells that are filled with the same tough protein found in nails and hair—acts as our armor plating, an effective barrier against light, heat, bacteria and many chemicals.

Below the epidermis lies the skin's middle layer of cells, the dermis. An elastic netting woven of two kinds of threads—a protein called collagen and a fiber known as elastin—the dermis gives the skin its strength and elasticity. This amazingly stretchable webbing allows our skin to expand over growing bellies and, in general, to snap back when the bulk shrinks. Within this dermal net are hair follicles, nerves, blood vessels, oil glands and sweat gland ducts.

The innermost layer of cells, the subcutaneous layer, attaches the elastic net to the underlying bone and muscle. Nerve endings, blood vessels and fat tissue are found in this layer.

WHAT HAPPENS TO SKIN AS WE AGE?

Changes in each skin layer ultimately influence what we see in the mirror every morning. And the age-related changes are more than skin deep:

- Below all three layers, *muscles* begin to deteriorate and lose their tone. Although much depends on how active we are, progressive loss of muscle and muscle tone generally goes along with age. Skin sags, puckers and creases as the muscles beneath it decrease in both volume and tone.

- *Fat* found in the innermost layer of the skin also decreases. Loss of subcutaneous fat affects the skin in the same way as loss of muscle: Skin sags and bags where once it was taut.

- In the skin's *innermost level*, the number of capillaries bringing oxygen and nutrients to the skin decreases, and arteries and veins become less efficient. Combined with the decreased volume of blood being pumped throughout the body—another age-associated change—this means the skin gets less and less nourishment. It loses its glow. It takes longer to repair itself.

- In the *middle layer* of cells, the netting of fibers that gives the skin its strength and elasticity gradually loses its oomph. Like the waistband of an old pair of gym shorts, the threads lose their ability to stretch and recover. The result is stiffer, less pliable skin that is less likely to snap back when we smile, scowl or squint.

- *Oil glands* become increasingly inactive as we age. Up to a point, that's good news for oily skin sufferers. But the upper layers of skin need the lubricating substance produced by the oil glands. Without it, the skin becomes dry and leathery. It creases and wrinkles with increasing ease.

- *Sweat glands* shrink, producing less and less sweat as we age. We lose our best natural moisturizer. Less sweat means the skin is a less efficient regulator of body temperature.

- In the skin's multi-tiered *top layer*, new skin cells aren't produced as quickly. It takes longer for us to heal. Fewer cells also mean thinner skin, which tends to wrinkle and crease easily and offers less protection against the environment.

- The top layer of skin loses some of the *pigment cells* that help protect us from the sun's damaging ultraviolet (UV) rays. Every decade from our late 20s to our mid 60s, we lose 20 percent of these pigment cells. Without their dark shield, the skin's inner layers become increasingly vulnerable to UV damage. When the rays penetrate to the middle layer of skin, they destroy the elastic fibers that give the skin its strength and stretchability. The damage is both cumulative and irreversible.

- Then there's *gravity*. Decades of being pulled earthward begin to catch up with us. When muscle tone is good and skin is elastic, the damage is minimal. But when we have a little sag here or there, gravity pulls at it relentlessly.

- *Life itself* conspires to give us wrinkles and sags. We grin, grimace and glower. We furrow our forehead, crinkle our nose, curl our lip. Each time we make a face, our skin folds and creases in a certain pattern. As we repeat the patterns, we gradually iron in the creases. In our 30s, as our skin becomes less resilient, we begin to experience the facial fallout from millions of smiles. A road map of our common expressions is etched on our faces.

AGE SPOTS

The helpful pigment cells that protect us from UV radiation are also responsible for those inevitable brown blotches known as age spots. Scientists are not sure how the process works, but they have some theories.

Some think the pigment cells, which tend to be fewer and larger the older one gets, cluster together—perhaps in response to repeated UV exposure. Others, notably Dr. Albert Kligman of the Clinic for Aging Skin, link age spots to the slowdown in cell renewal. Because cells divide more slowly, they remain in place longer, he explains. That means they have more chance to absorb dark coloring from the neighboring pigment cells.

Until researchers figure out exactly how age spots form, these discolorations will be a part of growing older. Prescription skin creams sometimes succeed in fading age spots, but over-the-counter preparations are generally too weak to have any effect at all.

NOT ALL SKIN IS CREATED EQUAL

Time captures some of us later than others. The skin of blacks, Asians and dark-complexioned whites is often slower to show the effects of age than that of their pale-skinned counterparts. That's because the protective pig-ment cells are more active in dark skin.

In general, men tend to wrinkle later in life than women, partly because men's skin starts out oilier than women's and partly because it's somewhat thicker, offering more protection. Some say regular shaving helps to keep men's skin younger-looking by scraping off dead skin cells and perhaps stimulating cell growth.

Heredity also plays a part in how quickly and in just what way our skin will age. But eventually, regardless of who we are, our skin will reflect the passage of years.

That's the bad news. Here's the good news: Much of what we think of as the effects of aging are really the results of *preventable* skin damage.

TEN AVOIDABLE ENEMIES OF YOUTHFUL SKIN

Researchers say that just about every skin change you can see with your eyes and feel with your hand is caused not by the natural aging process, but by exposure to damaging environmental factors—"environmental insults," they call them. And once skin is wrinkled, leathery or sagging, there is no cure. Costly treatments and sophisticated therapies can temporarily turn back the clock. But the smartest, healthiest, least expensive way to keep skin smooth and resilient is to avoid those things that prematurely age it. Here's the list:

1. **The sun**. Hiding in a closet all summer is not the answer—sunscreen is. Dermatologists suggest applying (and reapplying) sunscreen lotion with a protection factor of 15. (With this protection, your skin will react to 15 hours in the sun the way it would to one hour without sunscreen.) The lotion chemically absorbs the harmful rays. Another, messier option is zinc oxide, the white cream that decorates the noses of lifeguards. It protects by actually blocking and reflecting the rays. During the summer, skin needs protection on cloudy days as well as sunny ones because UV rays effectively penetrate cloud cover. Snow reflects and in-tensifies weak winter sunlight, making sunscreen a must.

OUR ENEMY, THE SUN

Basking in the sun may feel good, but skin specialists agree it's the single worst thing we can do to our skin. Tanned skin is not chic; it's *damaged*. Prolonged sunworshiping injures the skin—and the injuries are cumulative. Dermatologists say that years of working or luxuriating in the sun (without sunscreen protection) can make the skin look 15 to 20 years older than it is.

That's because the sun dries the skin into a tough leather, and dry skin wrinkles more easily and creases more deeply than normal skin. Long-term sun exposure can also cause blotches, discoloration, uneven thickness and irregular surface skin patterns. Perhaps worst of all, UV radiation destroys the elastic fibers that give the skin its strength and stretchability.

Scientists have ample proof of the sun's destructive power. When they examined the exposed facial skin of elderly people, they found that—no surprise—it looked, felt and acted like "old" skin. But when they examined the unexposed skin on the trunks of the same people, they found the skin had maintained its texture, tone and pliability.

Other researchers have scrutinized unexposed skin snipped from a variety of human rumps, finding no significant difference in thickness between the hide covering the rear of a 25-year-old and that of a 75-year-old. When another group of scientists tracked more than a dozen important measures of activity within skin cells, they found no difference between cells taken from a one-month-old baby and a 90-year-old woman—the unexposed skin cells, that is.

The environment is the culprit. The chief destroyer is the sun.

---

2. **Tanning booths**. Regardless of proclamations to the contrary, trendy indoor tanning beds emit the same, harmful rays as the sun. "Tanning in booths," says dermatology professor Dr. June Robinson of Northwestern University's Medical School, "poses

the same dermatologic risks as repeated solar exposure." In fact, the risks may be greater. Some booths are air cooled to keep customers comfortable. But tanners may be so cool and comfortable that they stay under the lights far too long.

3. **Wind.** For those who spend a great deal of time outdoors, wind poses a serious threat to youthful skin. It dries skin and toughens its texture. Faithful use of emollients and creams can keep pliable, undamaged skin moisturized and somewhat protected. But once skin is leathery, moisturizers can't appreciably soften it.

4. **Low humidity.** Hot or cold, indoors or out, dry air can prematurely age skin by robbing it of natural moisture and making it prone to wrinkles. In addition to using emollient lotions, skin specialists suggest plugging in a humidifier or placing an open pan of water on the radiator or stove.

5. **Tobacco.** The health consequences of smoking are so dire that it seems frivolous to mention tobacco's effect on the skin. But for those who need fresh reasons to quit smoking, here are some: Smoke wafting up from tip of the cigarette enshrouds the face, drying the skin and increasing the chance of wrinkles and lines. Nicotine constricts blood vessels, interfering with the full flow of nutrients to skin cells. It also robs the body of vitamin C—some say the equivalent of an orange for each cigarette smoked—a nutrient that helps the skin stay firm and elastic.

6. **Hot tubs and baths**. Taking a long, hot soak may relax muscles and ease tension, but it also dries the skin by washing away natural oils. The longer the soak, the more moisture the skin loses. To make matters worse, the water in public hot tubs (and public pools) is liberally laced with harsh disinfectant chemicals. Obviously necessary for public health reasons, these chemicals also dry the skin. Dermatologists are not only lukewarm about hot tubs, they're tepid on the subject of plain old bathtub bathing. Americans bathe too much, they say. They suggest relatively brief showers instead of baths, particularly during winter when the skin is already being accosted by dry air. For those who just can't give up a leisurely soak, they suggest using bath oils. Better yet, say some experts, apply moisturizer liberally after emerging from the bath and while still damp.

7. **Saunas.** Our skin loses both water and oil when we sit and sweat. When we emerge from the sauna (and obligatory cold dip or shower), our skin feels tight not because we've improved its texture or resiliency, but because we've dried it out.

8. **Diuretics** (water-reduction pills). Often abused by those who want

to lose weight fast, diuretics steal water from body tissue. For those who have problems with water retention, edema or hypertension, diuretics perform a healthful function. For others, all these pills do is dehydrate tissues, essentially drying the skin from the inside out.

9.   **Poor nutrition.** The whole body is affected by an unbalanced diet, but the skin may show it first. Lifeless, blotchy, excessively dry or oily skin may mean a deficiency in essential nutrients. Water—six to eight glasses a day—may also be vital to soft, young-looking skin.

FEEDING YOUR FACE

Forget fads. Megadosing on obscure trace minerals or slathering your face with liquid vitamin E is not the way to keep skin looking, feeling and acting young. Eating fresh, unprocessed, whole-grain food is. These ten nutrients are vital to healthy skin:

Nutrient	Effect on Skin	Food Source
vit. A	deficiency leads to dry, scaly, rough skin	leafy green vegetables, carrots, apricots, peaches
vit. C	prevents easy bruising of capillaries and blotchiness	green peppers, guavas, papayas, citrus fruits, tomatoes
vit. E	antioxidant; softens scar tissue	wheat germ, whole-grain bread, oatmeal, cooking oils
vit. B2	contributes to healthy working of oil glands	yogurt, milk, broccoli
niacin	deficiency leads to rough, red skin	liver, beef

Nutrient	Effect on Skin	Food Source
vit. B6	deficiency leads to excessively oily skin	wheat germ, bran, eggs, liver
EFAs	essential fatty acids help prevent dryness	fish, vegetable oils
iron	rich blood for maximum cell nourishment	liver, leafy green vegetables, peanuts
protein	building block of all tissues	fish, liver, meats, milk, legumes
zinc	deficiency leads to dry, scaly skin and impairs wound-healing	red meats, shellfish

10. **Sloth.** Inactivity is a formidable enemy. It robs us of muscle and bone mass, contributes to weight problems and, not incidentally, adversely affects the skin. Regular, vigorous exercise, on the other hand, not only helps control weight (lessening the chances of a host of problems), it also increases blood flow and bathes the skin in its natural moisturizer—sweat. Exercise may also help reduce the tension and stress that eventually etch the face with lines and creases.

AFTER THE DAMAGE IS DONE

It may be difficult to accept—especially when we're deluged by claims to the contrary—but the cumulative effects of sun, wind, gravity and years can't be permanently reversed. There is no cure for aging skin. We can stave off the damaging consequences of the environment—dryness, leathery texture, wrinkles and creases—but once the damage is done, it can't be permanently reversed. Here are some temporary solutions:

- *Moisturizers.* "Everyone should use a moisturizer," says University of Pennsylvania dermatologist Albert Kligman. But regardless of extravagant advertising claims, don't expect moisturizers to confer long-term benefits. They don't slow the skin's aging process. They temporarily soften dry skin and smooth superficial lines by furnishing water to the skin's outer layer and sealing it in. By cementing down the dry, dead cells of the skin's topmost tier, they give the skin a smoother feel. Superficial wrinkles, most obvious when the skin is dry, seem to flatten out when the skin's surface is moisturized. Exotic ingredients like DNA, elastin, collagen, mink oil or unpronounceable French formulas increase the cost of the product, but not its effectiveness. "Nothing's better than cold cream," says Dr. Kligman.

EXERCISING YOUR FACE

Will facial exercises keep your face fit? Proponents claim that systematically flexing and relaxing some of the more than four dozen facial muscles can give the skin "a facelift without surgery." They say facial exercises can cure sagging skin and smooth away wrinkles by enlarging underlying muscles.

Not so, say the experts. An American Medical Association study found that improving the tone of underlying muscles had no apparent effect on the outer skin layers. In fact, facial exercises may even do more harm than good, according to some dermatologists. Like facial expressions, exercises fold the skin into set patterns. Over time the folds become creases, and the creases become wrinkles. Ironically, exercises meant to smooth away wrinkles may actually create them.

- *Dermabrasion.* This procedure removes the skin's environmentally damaged upper layers by planing the face with a high speed brush, causing fine wrinkles to temporarily disappear. Performed in a doctor's office under local anesthetic, the procedure leaves the skin looking raw, then scabby for up to two weeks. Newly dermabraded skin may also be extremely sensitive to the sun for several months. But the biggest drawback to dermabrasion is the possibility of uneven pigmentation in those with dark or olive complexions.

- *The chemical peel.* Another, more painful way to get rid of the damaged top tiers of skin, this procedure temporarily erases lines, wrinkles and crow's-feet. A dermatologist or plastic surgeon paints the face with a caustic solution that causes a chemical burn. The harshness of the chemicals and the probability of pain requiring medication mean that the procedure is usually performed in a hospital. After the old skin is, in essence, burned and peeled off, new top tiers form to replace it. Meanwhile, for two weeks or so, the skin is raw, tender and scabby. As with dermabrasion, the chemical peel can result in permanent irregular skin pigmentation and so is not recommended for dark-skinned people.

SALON "FACE PEELS"

Here's the rule: If it sounds too good to be true, it usually is. "Face peels," touted by some beauty salons as conferring all the benefits of chemical peels at a fraction of the cost, may be ineffective, or worse yet—dangerous.

The American Medical Association has condemned the use of chemical peels by non-medical personnel, because some of the chemicals may cause permanent scarring if not used properly. On the other hand, weaker chemicals used by some salons give less satisfying results. And there's another drawback: Salon technicians may fail to feather the peeled area into the surrounding unpeeled area, leaving an obvious border between new and old skin.

The chemical peel is a serious procedure. Forget bargain hunting.

- *Collagen or silicone injections.* Doctors inject tiny beads of either substance under the skin, filling in the crevices and indentations that show up as wrinkles. Collagen injections do this "naturally" by replacing the skin's own damaged, weakened or lost collagen. Injections of silicone, an artificial substance, cause the body to build a network of its own collagen around the injected material. The problem with silicone injections, which are not FDA-approved (although the procedure is performed by some reputable dermatologists), is that this artificial substance may cause abscesses and other reactions and may migrate to other sites in the body. Either treatment can temporarily erase years of aging. But both are expensive, sometimes painful ordeals.

- *The facelift.* A major operation that takes two to three hours, the facelift gets rid of excess skin that has settled into wrinkles and bags, and pulls tight the remaining skin. A surgeon makes continuous cuts from the temple to the top of the ear and back into the hairline. Then the doctor separates the skin from the underlying muscle, pulls the skin up and back toward the ears, cuts off the excess and stitches together the incisions. This surgical reupholstery job costs between $2,000 and $5,000. The rejuvenating effects of a successful facelift will last about seven to ten years, say plastic surgeons. But for those with extremely sun-damaged skin, a facelift may last only a year or two.

HOPE FOR THE FUTURE

At his Clinic for Aging Skin in Philadelphia, Dr. Kligman has treated hundreds of people with vitamin A acid—which, unlike garden-variety vitamin A, is absorbed by the skin—and the unofficial results are encouraging. Kligman says regular applications of vitamin A acid, a prescription drug, increase blood flow, speed cell renewal and stimulate collagen and blood vessel formation in the skin's middle layer. Although he says it works best as a preventive measure applied to skin that is not already severely sun-damaged, vitamin A acid also seems to make older, sluggish, malfunctioning cells work well again.

Kligman intends to put vitamin A acid through rigorous, controlled testing as soon as a new, less irritating formulation is available, and it may be several years before his experiments are completed.

Meanwhile, other researchers are looking into the effects of certain kinds of essential fatty acids (EFAs). Some say eating foods rich in EFAs, like oily fish, or spreading EFAs directly on the skin may dramatically improve the texture, functioning and appearance of skin. Some studies have suggested the EFAs may improve the exchange of nutrients between cells and increase the skin's moisture-holding capacity. But concrete evidence is still years away.

5
Teeth

Teeth are unforgiving. They don't mend themselves like bones, clean themselves like eyes, heal themselves like skin or grow out like nails. Once broken, chipped, decayed or deeply stained, they stay that way.

All mammals—except humans—are blessed with continuously growing teeth that are gound down to size by the wear and tear of eating. Other animals have unlimited replacement teeth that pop up when needed throughout their lives. We must make do with only two sets of teeth, the second coming far too early in life for us to appreciate the gift.

Most of us take teeth for granted, brushing when we remember and dragging ourselves, sweaty-palmed and as infrequently as possible, to the dentist's office. We shouldn't be so cavalier. Teeth are much more than something to fill up a grin. They cut and grind food and mix it with saliva, performing the first, essential step in the digestive process. And, believe it or not, some researchers now think that teeth may be complicated sensory organs that provide us with a wealth of information about our environment. Thus those who—through bad genetic luck or bad habit—have weak, loose, misaligned or missing teeth may suffer from more than an imperfect smile.

WHAT HAPPENS TO TEETH AS WE AGE?

All of us, regardless of our dental diligence, will notice changes in our teeth as we age. Most of these changes are unwelcome, but one is a pleasant surprise: Teeth become less sensitive with age, as the size of the sensitive inner tooth pulp decreases and hard, dense, bone-like dentin takes its place. Dentists may even be able to drill older teeth without anesthesia.

What about the less pleasant changes:

- Teeth darken as dark, dense dentin takes the place of pulp inside the tooth. The enamel coating thins, allowing the darker underneath layer to show through.
- Teeth discolor from accumulated food, beverage and tobacco stains.
- Teeth wear away. Normal use doesn't pose much of a threat. In fact, scientists estimate that the current, normal rate of wear in teeth is so small they could serve us through almost three lifespans. But decades of incorrect brushing, teeth grinding, high acid diets or chronic vomiting (a symptom of bulimia) can wear them away far more quickly.
- Gums damage more easily and heal more slowly as the body's circulatory and immune systems slow down.
- Plaque—the invisible film of live bacteria that coats our teeth and gums—tends to accumulate faster with age and cause gum inflammation. Some blame the age-related decline in our immune system. Others point a finger at stressful lifestyles that seem to lower overall resistance.
- Teeth may become loose and unstable in their sockets as a result of gum disease or loss of jawbone density caused by osteoporosis (see Chapter 10).
- Because of plaque build-up and gum sensitivity, gum disease may take hold. This can result in anything from minor gum bleeding to major tooth loss.

PREGNANCY AND YOUR TEETH

"For every child, a tooth is lost," the old saying goes. While women need no longer fear a loss of teeth with an increase in family size, it is true that pregnancy can be hard on teeth and gums.

Hormonal changes during those nine months can exaggerate the gums' response to plaque. They may become easily irritated and swollen, receding from around the teeth and increasing the chances of gum disease. Gums may bleed because of this irritation or because increased blood volume during pregnancy puts additional pressure on delicate capillaries. It's also possible that the pregnant body responds less vigorously to certain oral bacteria, thus increasing the chances of tooth decay.

But excellent oral hygiene, modern dentistry, fluoridated water and proper nutrition can counteract these problems before they become serious. In addition to your daily brushing and flossing regimen, dentists strongly recommend a professional tooth-cleaning to counteract plaque buildup at least once during pregnancy. Nutritionists stress the increased need for both vitamin C to help gums heal quickly and calcium to protect bones (including the jawbone) from losing density.

Of all these, by far the most serious dental problem facing us in our early to late 30s is gum disease.

GUM DISEASE—THE PREVENTABLE EPIDEMIC

Cavities are not the root of oral evil—gum disease is. Responsible for 70 percent of all lost teeth, it attacks at least three out of four people in their mid-30s. More than 90 percent of all 65-year-olds have some form of gum disease. Yet this epidemic is the least treated of all dental problems. The American Society of Periodontology estimates that less than half of those who suffer from gum disease, even those with advanced cases, are seeking treatment.

Why? First, most adults, joyful that their days of five cavities per dental visit are over, assume that their worries have ended. They visit the dentist less frequently, if at all. In fact, the threat to their teeth at age 35 is far greater than at age 15. Second, the early symptoms of gum disease tend to go unnoticed, either because they are painless or because, like bleeding gums, they are thought of as "natural."

Plaque is the villain. This gummy, bacterial coating found in everyone's mouth accumulates on teeth beneath the gum line, where it is difficult to remove. And, regardless of concerted brushing and flossing, plaque faithfully reforms about every 24 hours. When it's not

THE SEVEN SIGNS OF GUM DISEASE

Gum disease, the quiet epidemic that eventually affects more than 90 percent of American mouths, often starts in the mid-30s. Because it begins slowly and painlessly, most people ignore the early symptoms. Don't. Watch for these changes:

1.   Gums that bleed when you brush your teeth
2.   Gums that are red, tender or swollen
3.   Gums that are pulling away from your teeth
4.   Infected pockets between your teeth and gums
5.   Permanent teeth that become loose.
6.   Any change in your bite
7.   Bad breath

removed daily, the bacteria grow, colonize and harden into calcified clumps when they die. These hardened deposits cause the gums to swell, redden, bleed and pull away from the teeth, allowing the plaque to penetrate deeper. The cycle continues: New spaces are created for plaque and debris to accumulate; gums continue to recede. The bacteria attack the area of the tooth exposed by the receding gums. They also go after the bone in which the teeth are moored. Untreated, gum disease causes teeth to loosen and fall out—or forces their removal.

But this ravager of millions of mouths is preventable. Dentists have evidence that most gum disease can be stopped by keeping teeth properly cleaned. You've heard the advice hundreds of times: brush, floss and see your dentist regularly. Now it's time to pay attention. The key to effective brushing is technique: Place the bristles at a 45 degree angle to the teeth so that they can slide beneath the gum line and get at the plaque. Flossing, which reaches areas between teeth and underneath gums that a brush cannot, is also a necessity.

But daily cleaning, no matter how thorough, won't completely prevent the formation of plaque, nor will it remove any hardened clumps attached to the teeth. For that, you need a professional cleaning by a dentist or dental hygienist. Most forms of gum disease respond to this simple, inexpensive treatment.

Gum disease sufferers once had only two choices. They could either do nothing, which meant losing their teeth and buying a new set (ten years ago, three out of five Americans over age 50 were totally toothless); or they could subject themselves to painful, expensive gum surgery, which might save some or all of the affected teeth.

Today, with pioneer researcher Dr. Paul H. Keyes leading the way, some dentists are suggesting another alternative. After spending 18 years at the National Institutes of Health studying gum disease in animals, Keyes concluded that better cleaning techniques coupled with close monitoring of bacterial growth could halt gum disease. In a study conducted at the National Institute of Dental Research, the Keyes method was used to treat 300 teeth with such advanced bone loss that other dentists felt they would have to be extracted. All but 10 were saved.

THE CONTROVERSIAL KEYES METHOD

Dr. Paul Keyes, a former government researcher who is now chairman of the board of the International Dental Health Foundation, shook the dental world when he insisted that oral surgery was not needed to cure most gum disease. The conservative, inexpensive treatment he and his followers recommend is still being hotly debated as the dental world awaits the scientific high sign: definitive results from long-term controlled studies.

Based on the belief that bacteria are the central cause of gum disease, the Keyes method involves detoxifying and disinfecting the mouth, making it an inhospitable place for germ life. The treatment begins in the dentist's office where all infected gum pockets are doused with an antiseptic solution, and plaque and tartar are removed.

Then, to keep bacteria from growing back and starting trouble, patients follow a rigorous, at-home program. After daily brushing and flossing, they use a Water Pik loaded with a salt solution. Then they work a paste of baking soda and hydrogen peroxide into the gums at the tooth line, brush with the leftover paste and rinse thoroughly with water.

At subsequent office visits, the dentist uses a microscope to monitor the success of the anti-bacterial battle. The cost for a total treatment of five to six visits? A relatively inexpensive $300 to $500.

Still, many specialists insist that the only way to cure advanced gum disease is surgery. The American Academy of Periodontology, the professional association for gum specialists, remains unconvinced that deep cleaning treatments are as effective as surgery. In some cases, they say, the pockets around the teeth are so deep, narrow or tortuous that it may be impossible to clean them thoroughly. Surgery makes it possible to get to the root and remove all the plaque.

PREVENTING CAVITIES

Adults seem to be less cavity-prone than kids—in part, no doubt, because most of the likely places are already filled with silver—but dental decay should still be of concern to the 30-year-old mouth. You get cavities when bacteria in your mouth ferment the sugars you eat, creating an acid that eats away at tooth enamel.

Aside from some unhappiness over the prospect of the silver surfaces outnumbering the enamel ones, why should you be concerned about tooth decay? Here are two good reasons:

- If you suffer from gum disease (like three out of four 35-year-olds), your gums are receding and exposing new areas of teeth to decay. The farther they recede, the more vulnerable the root becomes. Once the root decays, the tooth is no longer firmly attached to the bone.
- Any given tooth can only support so much silver. One cavity too many in a tooth makes it virtually impossible for the dentist to securely anchor the new filling. The result? A crown if you're lucky, extraction and possibly a false tooth if you're not.

However, it takes three things for decay to result: a susceptible tooth, a cavity-promoting diet and oral bacteria. That means you can employ a number of weapons in the war against decay. Our teeth can be made less susceptible through fluoride treatments or special sealants. (See "Prevention is the key," page 51.) Oral bacteria can be banished by a daily brushing and flossing routine, plus regular professional cleanings. Cavity-promoting diets can be changed. (See "You are what you chew," page 54.)

WHAT YOU NEED TO KNOW ABOUT TMJ

Another dental problem affects more than 10 million Americans and, although it can strike at any age, 20- to 40-year-olds are most frequently affected. The symptoms—headaches, earaches, sinus pain, muscle spasm—are often misdiagnosed as migraine, ear problems or allergies and treated ineffectively. The problem may actually be one of several complex dental conditions known collectively as TMJ disorders. (TMJ stands for temporomandibular joints—the hinges of the jaw.)

Under normal conditions, the jaw hinges work in harmony with five pairs of facial muscles to allow you to talk, chew and yawn. The system is an intricate one, and any single malfunction can disrupt it, beginning the cycle of TMJ disorders: muscle spasms, tenderness, pain, popping noises when you yawn and tissue damage.

Until recently all TMJ disorders were thought to be caused by problems with the way teeth fit together. Now researchers are finding it's not that simple. In fact, the most common TMJ disorder originates not with the jaw or the teeth but with the facial muscles. The cause? Stress. Victims—three times as many women as men are affected—tend to tighten their jaw muscles by clenching or grinding their teeth (a condition known as bruxism). Eventually this leads to muscle spasms and chronic facial discomfort.

Some TMJ disorders cure themselves with time. Others, once correctly diagnosed, may be treated with massage, moist heat applications, soft-food diets, biofeedback training and relaxation exercises. In severe cases, tranquilizers, muscle relaxants or even braces may be called for.

PREVENTION IS THE KEY

The old "drill, fill and bill" school of dentistry is gasping its last breath. Just about everyone is talking about preventive techniques as the way to keep teeth—and keep them looking good. Diligent oral hygiene and regular trips to the dentist are still the simplest and best ways to prevent gum disease and tooth decay, but there are some new twists.

FIVE STEPS TO ORAL HEALTH

Teeth: Ignore them and they'll go away. Despite the high-tech machinery and space-age materials of modern dentistry, the basic responsibility for keeping teeth healthy rests with the individual. Prevention is the key. Here's what the American Dental Association recommends:

1. Remove plaque by thoroughly brushing and flossing at least once a day. Use a soft bristle brush with rounded ends and a flat brushing surface. Angle the brush against the gum line and gently brush back and forth with short strokes. Use unwaxed floss (unless tightly spaced teeth make the waxed variety a necessity), and guide it between your teeth and up to the gum line. Curve it into a C shape against a tooth and gently slide it under the gum. Scrape the floss up and down against the side of the tooth.
2. Limit foods containing sugar, especially sticky sweets and sweets (like hard candy) that linger in the mouth. Remember that "healthy" food like dried fruits and fruit juices have sugar contents that rival junk food.
3. Eat a balanced diet to help maintain the gums and bones that support your teeth.
4. Use a fluoride toothpaste or gel. If your water is un-fluoridated, ask your dentist about fluoride tablets or other supplements. Fluoride actually does reduce the incidence of cavities.
5. Get regular checkups. Discovering a problem before it becomes serious generally means shorter, less costly treatments. The early stages of gum disease are so pain-less that most people don't know they're on the road to trouble unless they are professionally examined.

PICKING YOUR WAY TO ORAL HEALTH

The newest weapon in the war against gum disease is the one-and-a-half-inch sliver of wood that gives Emily Post fits: the toothpick. In two studies at the University of California, San Francisco, toothpicking proved to be a superior method for controlling plaque build-up and gum bleeding.

In one study, men and women with mild to moderate gum disease first brushed and flossed for two months, then added use of a toothpick for two months, and finally used the Keyes baking soda and peroxide paste mixture. After the toothpick phase, plaque and gum bleeding decreased 50 percent. The addition of the Keyes method caused no further improvement.

In the other study, dental students brushed and flossed one side of their mouths and brushed and picked the other. Signs of gum disease decreased significantly on the toothpicked side.

But don't go jabbing tender gums with pointy toothpicks. There's a method to correct picking. Use a sharp knife to make a slightly concave diagonal slice across the end of the toothpick. Insert it at a 45-degree angle to the tooth, down into the gum groove in front and in back of each tooth. Scrape gently. If you bleed, clean the area twice daily.

Dental technology is providing additional preventive aides. For those without fluoridated water or those who need extra help in the war against decay, there are ingestible fluoride tablets and fluoride solutions that can be painted directly on teeth. Fluoride helps prevent tooth decay by counteracting the enamel-eating acid regularly produced in the mouth.

Another decay-fighter is the application of dental sealants to certain tooth surfaces. An epoxy-like material, the sealant is used to fill tiny crevices in the enamel of a tooth. When the sealant hardens, the tooth has a smooth surface with no hiding places for food and bacteria. At a cost of $5 to $20 per tooth, the procedure seems to protect for up to five years.

YOU ARE WHAT YOU CHEW

"Hot things, sharp things, sweet things, cold things, all rot the teeth and make them look like old things," commented Ben Franklin back when dental technology consisted of a jigger of whiskey and a pair of pliers. He was right about sweet things, but it's not as simple as "sugar causes cavities." While all forms of sugar—from the "bad" sucrose found in candy to the "good" fructose found in fruits—are changed by bacteria in your mouth into tooth-decaying acids, the damage they do depends on how often and when you consume sugary foods, their consistency and how long they stay in your mouth.

You are most likely to get cavities:

- When you *regularly* eat sugary foods *between* meals. During mealtimes, the presence of other foods in your mouth apparently helps mitigate the action of sugar.
- When you eat sugary foods that *remain in your mouth* for a long time, such as hard candies, lollipops, cough drops or gum. They prolong the acid attack on teeth.
- When you *repeatedly sip* sugar-containing soft drinks, exposing teeth to a constant sugar bath. Dental researchers now believe that soft drinks may be just as likely to promote cavities as solid sweets, and that slow, between-meal sipping is far more harmful than consuming a whole drink at mealtime.
- When you eat *sticky sweets* that can remain on and between tooth surfaces for a prolonged period. This includes good food like raisins as well as guilt food like caramels. Dental researchers used to think stickiness was the single most important decay-deciding factor. Now they believe frequency and time in the mouth are equally or more important.

Sugar is the most popular villain, but not the only one. Sorbitol, xylitol and mannitol—popular sugar substitutes used in gums and mints—were until recently assumed harmless. Now new dental research has shown that these substances, like other sugars, can cause cavities, although at a slower rate.

Foods high in acid are also destructive to tooth enamel. Cola drinks and fruit juices may be particularly harmful, because they combine high acid content with high sugar levels and are often sipped over a long period of time. Although an apple a day doesn't really keep the doctor (or dentist) away, it is far better for your teeth to eat whole fruit than its juice. In general, the juice is more acidic that the fruit from which it was extracted. And it doesn't contain the fibrous content of the fruit, which stimulates the flow of saliva and helps clean debris from the mouth.

Food high in phosphorus can set off a chain of biochemical events harmful to your teeth and gums, especially if your calcium intake is low. Red meat, poultry, fish, flour and carbonated soft drinks are all loaded with phosphorus, and an excess of phosphorus signals the body to "steal" calcium from its bones to maintain a metabolic balance. Bone loss in the jaw is major factor in gum disease.

But dental health involves more than cutting down on certain foods. You can take a positive approach by including these beneficial foods in your diet:

- Leafy green vegetables, fruits and other foods high in vitamin C. Vitamin C keeps gums healthy and helps fight bacterial invasions.
- Milk, yogurt, cheese and other foods high in calcium. Calcium keeps the jawbone strong and dense so that teeth are anchored securely.
- Aged cheddar, Swiss and Monterey Jack cheeses. Recent research suggests that these cheeses fight decay by preventing sugar from fermenting into decay-causing agents.
- Wheat germ, bran, peanuts and walnuts. They appear to act as buffers against acid in the mouth.
- Sage and garlic. Recent research suggests that they inhibit the fermentation of sugars into acid.

NEW TECHNIQUES FOR BETTER, BRIGHTER TEETH

A painless process that makes stained and discolored teeth white again? A technique one-third the cost of capping that restores chipped, cracked or uneven teeth? Yes—it's called *bonding*. The less-than-perfect tooth is first etched with a mild acid gel to roughen its surface. Then a putty-like resin material, mixed to match the desired color, is applied over the tooth, where it immediately bonds to the enamel. The dentist sculptures the material to the appropriate shape before hardening it with a beam of light. Your smile reveals a completely natural-looking tooth.

Although some dentists are wary of this new technique, pointing out that bonded teeth seem to stain easily and that the treatment is less permanent than capping, many are enthusiastic. Bonding involves no anesthetic and can often be completed in one visit.

For crooked, misaligned teeth, new *high-tech braces* may be the answer. Today almost 20 percent of all orthodontic patients are adults, and most are not sporting "tin grins" or "tinsel teeth." That's because much of the metallic hardware common to old-fashioned braces has been replaced by transparent or tooth-colored plastics and thinner wires. Some people are able to wear state-of-the-art "invisible" or hidden braces that attach to the backs of the teeth. Others can be fitted with removable appliances that need only be worn at night.

Adults are bracing up not only to improve their smiles, but to cure painful TMJ disorders caused by misalignment and to make their mouths less susceptible to gum disease. But there's a catch: Correcting misaligned teeth in adults is not as simple as it is in children, whose still-growing teeth and jaws can be easily altered.

Adult braces may have to be worn for a longer time, and tooth extraction or jaw surgery is sometimes necessary. Straightened, aligned teeth are easier to clean and thus less susceptible to decay and gumline plaque build-up. But, ironically, the act of straightening may itself contribute to gum disease. Braces sometimes make it difficult to brush effectively, with food debris and bacteria lodging in the hardware and under the gumline. And then there's the cost, which ranges from expensive to outrageous.

If your mouth is beyond the the help of both bonding and braces, you may be interested in another recent technological breakthrough, *dental implants*. Considered one of the most significant dental developments in our lifetime, these permanently anchored false teeth are quickly making bridges and dentures obsolete. Designed to look as much like real teeth as possible, implants can be surgically attached to remaining root and bone tissue, or to metal plates inserted in the jawbone.

TOMORROW'S CURES

Scientific and technological discoveries are changing dentistry and could soon change the way we care for our teeth. These innovations should help us keep our teeth looking young and functioning well for a lifetime.

- **Plaque-dissolving agents.** A major cause of oral health problems that is directly linked to gum disease, plaque is the dental profession's number-one target. For years researchers have been seeking a way to dissolve plaque with toothpastes and mouth rinses—and in a few more years, such products may be available. In some European countries, chlorhexedrine mouthwashes have been used successfully to prevent plaque formation.
- **Anti-cavity vaccine.** Pop a pill to prevent tooth decay? Researchers are cautiously optimistic about the possibility. Now that they are beginning to understand the decay process, they're learning how to interfere with it. Extensive experimentation in the United States and Europe has revealed that immunization with the bacteria that cause tooth decay produces antibodies that work well in reducing cavity formation.
- **Time-release fluorides.** Scientists at the National Institute of Dental Research are currently experimenting with a device they believe will make a major contribution to preventive dentistry. It's a small fluoride pellet that is attached to the side of a molar with the same cement used to affix braces. A thin plastic coating on the pellet allows the continuous release of fluoride into the mouth. In tests on laboratory animals, those with the pellets had less than half the cavities than those without. The pellets should be on the market within four years.
- **Laser technology.** Another potential tool in preventive dentistry, the laser is being tested by two Canadian researchers. They envision a variety of uses from smoothing the surface of the teeth to getting rid of bacteria-holding crevices to destroying root canal infections without surgery.
- **Genetically engineered fillings.** Researchers are currently using gene-cloning techniques to produce tooth enamel in mice and have isolated one of the four enamel genes in humans. If they can isolate the other three and solve a few minor problems, they may come up with a filling substance similar to natural enamel in appearance, structure and durability.

But for now, the responsibility for a bright, appealing, disease-free mouth is ours. And there is no reason other than neglect for age to diminish our smile.

6

Fat

Thunder thighs, saddlebags and love handles. Spare tires, beer bellies, double chins and jowls. Some 40 million Americans tip the scales at 20 percent above their ideal weight, carting around enough excess baggage to cramp their lifestyles and threaten their health. It seems that every year past 30, another pound or two takes up permanent residence where we least need it.

More than 75 million of us are weary warriors in the battle of the bulge. Thirteen million have enrolled in Weight Watchers. Another ten million pop over-the-counter diet pills, spending more than $250 million a year. But studies show that less than one dieter in ten is able to lose 20 pounds and keep it off for a year. And the battle seems to get harder as we get older.

It's as if our bodies were designed to make weight gain inevitable and weight loss impossible. Consider these facts: Fat cells in the body are easily created and never die; fat cells require very little energy to maintain themselves.

From the time we are born until the time we die, we can add fat cells under the skin, within tissues and around vessels and organs. But, regardless of diet or exercise regimens, regardless of pounds lost or inches shrunk, we never rid ourselves of a single fat cell. Individual fat cells may shrink in size, but they are still there waiting to plump up again.

Not only do they stay with us forever, but they need far fewer calories to stay alive than muscle cells. That means the more fat cells we have, the less we need to eat to keep our bodies going. And that means we don't have to overeat to gain weight. In fact, once we've gained enough fat, we can eat the *same* number of calories—or even reduce the number of calories—and continue to add fat cells. So each year we gain a little more weight until, at 35, 40, or 50, we have a problem.

And the problem is not just an aesthetic one. Those of us who are more than 20 percent above ideal weight with more than 30 percent of our total weight coming from fat, run the risk of a number of health problems. Excess weight can overtax the heart and put undue stress on the back and weight-bearing joints like knees and ankles. It can affect blood vessels, contributing to high blood pressure and varicose veins. It can elevate blood cholesterol levels, the leading risk factor in heart disease. It can increase the chance of developing diabetes and kidney disease. Recent studies also associate obesity with an increased risk of cancer of the breast, colon, uterus and gallbladder.

Does advancing age have to mean increasing weight? Is "middle-age spread" inevitable? Our bathroom scales may say yes, but researchers say no.

WHAT HAPPENS AS WE AGE

At first glance, results from a number of scientific studies seem depressing. Here's what researchers have found:

- Weight increases in the middle years, with fat deposits under the skin increasing progressively from the third decade on.
- Men reach their maximum weight between 34-54; women continue gaining into their 60s.
- Women deposit more fat and maintain it longer than men.
- Body composition changes. At 25, a man's body is about one-fifth fat. At 70, fat accounts for more than one-third of the body. Lean tissue, almost one-half the body at 25, decreases to one-third at 70.
- Older bodies, in general, burn fewer calories. Basal metabolism (the rate at which the body burns calories when at rest) decreases with age. A 30-year-old man uses 1,600 calories to maintain body functions. An 80-year-old man uses 25 percent fewer calories.

There is a bright side to all this. Although these changes are associated with growing older, none is an inescapable consequence of aging. Weight, fat deposit, body composition and metabolic changes are largely within our control.

Most people think increasing age brings with it a sluggish metabolism, and they blame this slow-down for middle-aged spread. Not so, say National Institute of Aging researchers. They did find slower metabolisms in older people, but they discovered that diminishing muscle mass, not age, was responsible. Remember that muscle cells consume far more energy than fat cells. Fewer muscle cells mean fewer calories burned and a lower metabolism, at work or at rest.

Do we naturally lose muscle mass as we age? No. We lose it because we don't use it. Does our thirtieth birthday signal the beginning of an inevitable shift in the fat-to-muscle ratio? No. The increasingly sedentary lifestyle often associated with getting older causes this shift.

THE CALORIES YOU BURN

What determines the number of calories you burn each day? Here's a list of important factors:

- **Body size**. Big bodies take more energy to operate than small bodies.
- **Body composition**. People with high percentages of lean tissue burn more calories than those with high percentages of fat.
- **Gender**. Women burn fewer calories than men because their percentage of body fat is higher.
- **Activity level**. Active people burn more calories than sedentary people both while exercising and for up to 24 hours afterward.
- **Setpoint**. It may be that every body is programmed to burn calories and store fat according to a predetermined schedule or quota.
- **Emotions**. Tense people burn more calories than their calm counterparts
- **Temperature**. People burn more calories when exposed to extremes of heat and cold than in temperate climates.

All the research points to one key for controlling weight gain and fat build-up as we age: regular exercise. But what do most people do when they want to lose weight? They diet.

YOU CAN NEVER BE TOO RICH OR TOO THIN

We are a diet-obsessed nation. Certainly there are millions who need to lose weight. But there are also millions who only imagine they need to. Compulsive and continuous dieting, not to mention eating disorders like anorexia and bulimia, show that some of us will do anything to pare our bodies down to the currently desirable silhouette. But is being underweight really desirable? The research is contradictory.

Scientists have been looking into the effects of undernutrition since the 1930s. These studies—rats and mice have been the subjects, not humans—indicate almost unequivocally that carefully controlled food restriction with adequate vitamins and minerals slows the aging process. In experiment after experiment, thin animals consistently outlive their all-you-can-eat cousins, sometimes doubling their average life span. They seem to age more slowly too. The level of cholesterol in their blood stays lower longer; their bodies stay responsive to certain hormones longer; their immune systems stay healthier longer. Underfed rodents are also less likely to suffer from age-related diseases like cancer, and kidney and heart disease.

But the effect of scientifically controlled undernutrition on people is unknown. For obvious ethical reasons, no human beings have been purposefully underfed for the greater good of science. Instead, researchers have kept tabs on large numbers of people, correlating their weight with their health over long periods of time. And, in direct contrast to the laboratory experiments, these population studies suggest that being underweight can actually be dangerous to your health. It may not be possible to be too rich, but one apparently can be too thin.

In a major National Institutes of Health study that followed more than 5,000 men and women for 24 years, scientists discovered that the thinnest people ran the greatest risk of dying. The leanest group of men had the highest death rates from cancer and all other diseases except those of the cardiovascular system. A new study from the group that publishes those "ideal weight" charts we measure ourselves against also finds that thinness doesn't mean wellness. Men 15 percent below average weight die more often from pneumonia, influenza, hypertensive heart disease and suicide than their weightier counterparts, according to the study. Women 15 percent less than average are vulnerable to pneumonia, influenza and digestive-system diseases. An American Cancer Society study found that those 20 percent underweight died more often from strokes and digestive diseases than their average-weight counterparts. In a California study of 7,000 men and women, the highest death rates were among those 10 percent underweight.

Conversely, these and other studies are finding that being slightly or moderately overweight—even as much as 35 percent above standard weight chart "ideals" in one study—is good for your health. But will fashion ever follow health? Today the look remains lean (although not as emaciated as has been the ideal in previous years), and millions diet to achieve it.

IN SEARCH OF THE PERFECT DIET

Wonder diets appear monthly. Diet gurus write momentary bestsellers and take to the talk-show circuit, each claiming to have discovered *the* way to shed and keep off pounds. Just how good are these mass-market diets? Dr. Paul Lachance, the first nutritionist for the space program and now professor of food science and nutrition at Rutgers University, answered this question in an article in *Consumer's Digest*. He and a colleague evaluated more than a dozen popular diets according to their balance of protein, carbohydrate and fat, their vitamin, mineral and fiber content, and their levels of sodium and cholesterol.

The Pritikin diet, says Lachance, is "good but very lean" with its nine percent fat content. The Simmons and I Love New York diets get "fair" ratings. Both the Stillman and Atkins diets, he says, have too little fiber and too much fat, including five times the recommended intake of cholesterol. But the plan Lachance rates lowest is the infamous Beverly Hills diet, because it provides low-quality protein and negligible amounts of calcium, iron and other vital nutrients.

Fads and Gimmicks

Fad weight-loss schemes promising instant, dramatic results have ensnared many miracle-hunting dieters. Plans consisting of all one food—grapefruit, for example—are dangerously unbalanced, deprive the body of essential nutrients and generally cause loss of water and muscle, not fat. The fact is that no food or combination of foods will burn off unwanted body fat. Extreme low-calorie diets like the 400-calorie-a-day original Cambridge liquid diet pose "definite health risks," according to Lachance. At the height of the diet's popularity in the early 1980s, it killed six people, according to the FDA. Another 138 reported various symptoms. Earlier liquid-protein diets—one ironically marketed as the "the last diet you'll ever need"—were the last diets at least 58 people needed. That's the number of recorded deaths linked to these once popular get-slim-quick regimens.

Lust for leanness sometimes causes people to believe the unbelievable. Hundreds of slimness seekers once sent away for appetite-suppressing eyeglasses with colored lenses that were supposed to project an image on the retina that dampened the desire to eat. (Authorities stepped in and stopped the scam.) Thousands invest in creams, gels, wraps, belts and suits that promise quick weight loss. Pounds are shed, but the weight loss is entirely water (sweat), and it is only temporary. As soon as the salve-slathered or sauna-suited dieter drinks a glass of water to replenish lost liquid, the scales tip back. Others in search of quick and easy weight loss have turned to electric muscle stimulators, legitimate devices in physical therapy but useless for weight loss or figure firming.

Pills

Another popular, generally wrong-headed approach to losing weight is pill popping. One recent scam involved a miraculous pill that allowed the user to eat all the pasta and bread he or she wanted without gaining an ounce—or so the various manufacturers of "starch blockers" claimed. Neither the pills' effectiveness nor safety was ever proved. The FDA banned them and is still investigating medical complaints. Another substance called *glucomannan* is advertised as an "Oriental weight-loss secret." But it's merely a source of fiber (like the ordinary, far less expensive of grains, vegetables and fruit) that creates a mild feeling of fullness.

Desperate dieters, with the help of an agreeable doctor or the neighborhood drug dealer, sometimes turn to amphetamines. These prescription-only appetite suppressants are highly addictive and can have serious, adverse effects on the heart and central nervous system.

But the most popular kind of diet pills are sold over the counter, and millions of Americans, most of them women, spend hundreds of millions of dollars on them each year. The major ingredient in these preparations is phenylpropanolamine (PPA), a controversial, laboratory-produced chemical similar to adrenaline. Various studies show that PPA is effective as a mild appetite curber, but researchers continue to debate its safety. About 10,000 people reported having problems with PPA in 1981, including dizziness, restlessness, insomnia, headaches, vomiting, nausea and heart palpitations, according to the national clearinghouse for Poison Control Centers. An Australian study linked seizures, kidney failure, chest pains and psychotic episodes to PPA use in some people.

Some diet pills also contain caffeine, meant to relieve the fatigue that often accompanies reducing diets. Others contain diuretics that promote water loss. Most diet gum or candy contains benzocaine, a mild local anesthetic that numbs the taste buds.

The Perfect Diet

Forget fads, gimmicks and pills. Forget claims of ultimate diets, instant fat burners and overnight weight loss. At best, these tricks help with temporary weight loss. At worst, they cause harm. At any rate, they don't teach you how to eat for long-term weight control. Nutritionists agree that a balanced diet rich in complex carbohydrates (cereal, bread, grain), low in fats (whole dairy products, oils, eggs, nuts) and devoid of refined sugars (cakes and cookies) is the way to go. Reducing fat intake from the current average of 40 percent of calories down to 20 percent or lower helps control weight as it guards against heart disease. A common recommendation for daily eating is four servings of fruits and vegetables; four servings of breads, cereals and grains; two servings of dairy products; and two servings of poultry, fish or lean meat.

For those who feel they must follow a diet plan, Dr. Lachance rates the low-fat, high-carbohydrate "F-Plan" diet "near perfect." A weight-loss regimen based on the work of a noted British physician, it was popularized in the U.S. by a 1983 paperback. He also likes the venerable Weight Watchers diet for its good balance and high vitamin and mineral content.

WHY DIETS DON'T WORK

More than 90 percent of those who diet are unsuccessful. Either they can't lose weight or they can't keep it off. Are they all weak-willed closet snackers? Do they all binge on weekends? Of course not. Many people—maybe you—are devoted dieters who play by all the rules and still can't win. Why?

Today's psychologists specializing in weight counseling say that diets simply don't get at the root of a person's relationship to food. Issues like self-esteem and personal power can affect eating behavior in ways too deep for a diet to touch. Nutritionists have said for years that "going on a diet" is a poor approach to permanent weight loss. A diet, any diet, is an abnormal (to the dieter) eating plan adopted for a specific period. Assuming the plan works and pounds are lost, the overjoyed dieter stops dieting and, almost inevitably, returns to his or her normal eating habits—those same habits that may have been responsible for weight gain in the first place. Not surprisingly, in a matter of weeks the dieter regains all the lost weight.

But what about people who can't seem to lose more than a pound or two, regardless of how many calories they cut? In fact, they complain that the fewer calories they consume, the less weight they lose. And they're right. Here's the explanation: When the body is deprived of calories, it reacts by slowing down its internal processes (that is, by lowering its metabolism) to save energy. It acts to protect and preserve itself in the event of long-term deprivation or starvation. The body cannot tell the difference between starvation and dieting. So the act of dieting itself, expecially when the dieter severely limits calories, is essentially self-defeating: The fewer calories you eat, the lower your metabolism, the fewer calories you need, the more your body stores as fat.

The idea that the body regulates its use and storage of energy (fat) according to its own schedule—overriding your concerted attempts to change that schedule through dieting—is at the heart of a new, increasingly popular theory. It's called "setpoint," and it speculates that every body has a built-in control system dictating how much fat it should carry. Researchers do not yet know what combination of heredity and environment determines each person's setpoint, but evidence is mounting that each human body demands an amount of fat tissue that can vary widely from person to person. This explains the seemingly contradictory observation made by a variety of researchers: Most fat people don't eat more than most thin people.

How do overweight people get fat when they don't eat more? How do they stay fat even when dieting furiously? They have a high setpoint. Their bodies are pre-programmed to store more fat, regardless of what they eat, than a thin person's. Scientists think that the brain learns about the state of the body's stores of fat through chemical messages, some of which are sent by the fat cells themselves. When fat stores fall below a certain level—let's say you've successfully shed a few pounds—the body reacts by craving more calories and storing more fat. You eat more; your metabolism slows, and soon you're back to the weight your body is pre-set to maintain.

The key to weight control, say researchers, is changing the setpoint, not battling it. Dieting doesn't budge it but instead attempts—unsuccessfully—to overpower it. But those with high setpoints are not doomed to spend their lives carrying around excess weight. Exercise, say some researchers, can lower the setpoint and decrease the amount of fat we're programmed to store.

EXERCISE

A renowned nutritionist tells this story: An overweight woman went to her doctor and asked for a prescription for amphetamines to help her lose weight. The doctor whipped out his prescription pad, scrawled "Adidas" across it, tore off the page and handed it to her. The woman, so the story goes, embarked on a daily walking program, lost the weight she needed to and now won't miss a day of exercise.

Exercise is not a fad, nor is it something we can forego as we grow older. It is, in fact, the key to lifelong weight control. Everyone knows that exercise itself burns calories, but consider these additional weight-loss benefits of regular, sustained physical activity:

- Exercising increases the rate at which we burn calories *after* we stop the activity. University of New Hampshire researchers found that aerobic exercise kept metabolic rates higher than normal for up to 24 hours after exercising.
- Exercising helps increase and maintain muscle tissue as it decreases fat stores. Because muscle cells are more metabolically active

(require more calories to stay alive) than fat, lean people naturally burn more calories than fat people even when they're not engaged in activity.

- Exercising may help lower the body's setpoint, that pre-programmed level of fat the body strives to maintain despite the number of calories taken in.

EXERCISE AND CALORIE EXPENDITURE

According to data compiled by the National Institutes of Health, a 150-pound person would burn the following number of calories when engaged in the activities below:

Activity (one hour)	Calories burned
Running 10 mph	1,280
Jogging 7 mph	920
Jumping rope	750
Jogging 5 1/2 mph	740
Cross-country skiing	700
Running in place	650
Swimming 50 yds/min	500
Walking 4 1/2 mph	440
Bicycling 12 mph	410
Tennis (singles)	400
Walking 3 mph	320

A 100-pound person will burn one-third fewer calories than those shown on the chart. A 200-pound person will burn one-third more.

Of course, exercise is far more than a way to remain trim. It is vital to the health of heart and lungs, helps prevent high blood pressure and age-related loss of bone mass (osteoporosis), and increases our strength, endurance, flexibility and coordination. Researchers estimate that half of the functional decline attributed to age is really the result of *dis-use*—inactivity.

Anything that gets you moving, from lawn mowing to slalom skiing, is exercise, but experts agree that *aerobic* exercise is best for both weight control and cardiovascular health. Any activity that involves movement vigorous, constant and prolonged enough to work the heart, lungs and circulatory system so that they demand large amounts of oxygen is considered aerobic. A Sunday game of touch football with its stop and go action is not aerobic. A brisk hike is. The top aerobic activities include cross-country skiing, running, swimming, bicycling, rope-jumping, brisk walking and aerobic dance. Those who lift weights, bowl, golf or play most team sports may be reaping other benefits, but their activities are not aerobic.

Experts say you should engage in aerobic activity for 20 to 45 minutes, three to five times a week. The key is exercising hard enough to elevate your heartbeat to training level, but not so hard that you can't maintain constant activity.

YOUR TARGET PULSE RATE FOR AEROBIC EXERCISE

How hard should you exercise? To get the maximum aerobic and weight-control benefits, maintain the pulse rate listed for your age for at least 20 minutes, at least three times a week.

Age	Pulse range
30	143-162
32	142-161
34	140-159
36	140-158
38	138-156
40	137-155
45	134-152
46-50	130-146
51-55	128-142
56-60	120-138
61-65	113-133
66-70	105-128

This chart is an accurate guide if your resting heart rate is near the average of 80 beats per minute for women or 72 beats a minute for men. But if your heart beats considerably slower than this, the upper range shown on the chart may be too high. To figure your own optimum exercise pulse rate:

1. Calculate your resting heart rate by taking your pulse in the morning before exercise.
2. Calculate your maximum heart rate by subtracting your age from 220.
3. Use this formula: (Maximum − resting) × .65 + resting = your exercise pulse rate.

Here's how the formula works for a 33-year-old man with a resting heart rate of 60. Maximum rate is $(220 - 33)$ 187.

$$(187 - 60) \times .65 + 60 = 142$$

You don't have to be a triathlete to stay in shape. Research indicates that even moderate levels of activity like brisk walking can control weight. In one study, older people who took daily walks lost 80 percent of the under-the-skin fat they had accumulated since early adulthood, while increasing both lean tissue and bone calcium.

Part III
GOOD SENSES

7

Sight

From the moment we squint at the alarm clock to the time we blearily set down the bedtime book, we depend on them. They may weigh only a quarter of an ounce and measure a scant inch in diameter, but our eyes are responsible for bringing us 90 percent of the information we use each day.

Scientists think of them as electro-chemical pathways to the brain. Nutritionists consider them sensitive barometers of diet. Some doctors claim they are miniature maps of the body. Poets herald them as windows to the soul. But to the rest of us, eyes are merely interesting facial features We think more about their color and shape than we do about their function—until they begin to give us trouble.

Which they invariably do as we grow older. In fact, no other human organ reflects the process of aging more readily than the eye. But although changes begin in our mid-20s, they don't catch up with us until our 40s or later. And even then—thanks to breakthroughs from lasers to lens technology—most sight-damaging problems can be treated and corrected. Eyes do show the ravages of time, but a lifetime of clear sight is possible if we treat our eyes well.

WHAT HAPPENS TO EYES AS WE AGE

One day we read the morning paper as usual. The next, the words blur before our eyes. Although we sometimes experience change suddenly, most sight-related problems are actually a long time coming.

And they come to everyone. Even though you may be seeing crisply without the aid of glasses or contacts, the following age-related changes are beginning:

- *The white of the eye* becomes less white as blood vessels become prominent and mineral deposits form. Years of exposure to environmental irritants, from sunlight to industrial pollutants, can cause (harmless) yellow patches to form near the iris.
- *The iris*, the colorful ring of muscle that opens and closes the pupil, begins to fade. The pigment cells that give younger people vivid eye coloring gradually migrate from the iris through minuscule canals that normally carry eye fluid. This paling of the eyes doesn't itself affect eyesight, but the migrating pigment can clog the canals, which may contribute to glaucoma.
- *The cornea*, the transparent window in front of the iris, begins to flatten out. This may either create or worsen astigmatism, an often correctable condition that causes varying degrees of visual distortion.
- *The lens*, transparent and flexible in our youth, begins to cloud and harden. Its lack of transparency means less light reaches the retina, and we see a dimmer image. Hardening also means difficulty in focusing, especially on close objects.
- *The eye muscles*, like other muscles in the body, begin to lose their elasticity. Out ability to track objects quickly and precisely begins to suffer when the six major muscles that move the eyeball lose some of their tone.
- *The retina*, the back-of-the-eye screen that absorbs light and changes it into electrical impulses to be interpreted by the brain, also changes with age. If the blood supply is restricted because of hardened or blocked arteries, patches of retinal tissue may die. The result: blind spots.
- *The optic nerve*, the conduit between the eye and the brain, undergoes relatively mild, unimportant age-related changes. But if the arteries nourishing the nerve become hardened or blocked, the nerve itself may atrophy and die. Depending on the extent of the damage, anything from mild visual impairment to blindness may result.

Although the litany of changes sounds gloomy, the fact is that most of us—if we practice preventive care and seek prompt treatment—will to through life with nothing more harrowing to contend with than a pair of bifocals.

AGING AROUND THE EYES

Years before we notice the results of any of the structural changes that can affect how we see, we notice another change, completely harmless yet sometimes psychologically devastating: We begin to look older "around the eyes." In fact, crow's-feet and bags under the eyes are often the first signs of aging. Puffiness, circles under the eye and crinkled eyelids are other unwelcome reminders of the passage of time.

The skin around the eyes is frequently the first to go because it is thin, exposed to the environment and subject to the extensive mechanical stress of blinking, squinting and contributing to facial expressions. The upper eyelids contain no moisturizing oil glands, making them prime candidates for drying and wrinkling. The skin under the eyes, on the other hand, tends to retain oil and has a tendency to puff up. Age-weakened muscle tone plus loss of skin elasticity and subcutaneous fat cause bags under the eyes. (For a full discussion on how and why the skin ages, see Chapter 4.)

Because damage to the skin is both cumulative and irreversible, preventive care is the key. Following these suggestions can help keep the skin around your eyes looking youthful:

- Use a substantial sunscreen (protection factor 15) whenever you go outside. The sun is your skin's worst enemy.
- Use a moisturizer—heavy on the eyelid, lighter on the under-eye—night and day. Dry skin wrinkles more quickly and more deeply than moisturized skin.
- Don't smoke. It dries your skin, makes you squint (thus imprinting crow's-feet) and robs your body of vitamin C.
- Get enough sleep. The skin around your eyes is so delicate that it responds immediately to fatigue and stress.
- Don't rub your eyes. Rubbing stretches the thin eye skin and encourages bags.

For those whose mirrors have already surprised them with reflections of wrinkled, baggy skin around the eyes, there is help. Collagen injections lessen crow's-feet (see Chapter 4), and cosmetic surgery can take up slack skin and erase bags. A relatively simple procedure considered one of the most reliable plastic surgery operations, "eyelifts" can be performed in a doctor's office under local anesthetic.

EYE STRAIN

As we move into our 30s and 40s we may begin to experience headaches, temporarily sore and itchy eyes and eye fatigue—not because we're growing older but because we're working longer and harder. Tired, aching eyes are a sign that we've pushed our eye muscles too far. It's the muscles surrounding the eye, not the eyeball itself, that become strained.

VDTs (video display terminals), now a part of so many workplaces, are considered a major culprit. According to a National Academy of Science study, there is no scientific evidence that eye disease, cataracts or other forms of visual damage result from working with VDTs. But temporary visual difficulties ranging from headaches to blurred vision are well-documented. And the more time spent at the computer, the greater the chance of problems. To lessen the risk or severity of eyestrain, position yourself or the screen to avoid glare, don't hunch over the keyboard, and be sure to take frequent visual breaks by focusing on faraway objects. Daily relaxation exercises may also help.

FOUR STRESS AND STRAIN REDUCERS FROM CHINA

Piles of paperwork or hours in front of the computer screen can be tough on your eyes. Headaches, eyestrain and eye irritation are common afflictions among desk jockeys and others who do close work. To rest your eyes and relieve strain and tension, the Chinese have developed some simple exercises that stimulate acupressure points. While western doctors may be skeptical about these techniques, millions of Chinese swear by them.

Before you begin this series of four exercises, shut your eyes and cover them with your palms, the lower palm resting on your cheekbone. Rest your elbows on a desk or table and relax for a minute or two, then remove your palms.

Now you're ready to try the acupressure exercises. It may take some practice to hit the right spots. Concentrate. The acupressure points are slightly more sensitive than the surrounding skin:

1. *Points under the eyebrows.* Resting a bent forefinger and middle finger of each hand against your forehead, use your thumbs to gently press and rub two points just under the eyebrows near the bridge of the nose. You'll feel them as indentations in the bone that forms the top of your eye socket. Rub toward the inside several times, then the outside. Repeat.
2. *Points on either side of the nose.* Use the thumb and forefinger of either hand to press and squeeze two points on either side of your nose just below your eyes. Press down, then squeeze up. Repeat.
3. *Points around the eye socket.* Make fists and place them against the eyebrows with your thumbs at the temples. Rub all round the eye sockets several times with the middle joint of the forefinger. Some acupressurists recommend stimulating these points one by one with a small clockwise motion of the index finger.
4. *Points below the eye.* Hook your thumbs under your chin and place both forefingers just below the eyes, along the bony ridge halfway between the nose and the far end of the eye. Rub toward the inside, then toward the outside. Repeat.

Whether or not you hit the correct acupressure points each time, your eyes will benefit from the gentle massage and the respite from close work. End the exercises by "palming" your eyes for a minute or two; then stare off at a distant point for another minute or two.

If problems persist, you might consider a new pair of glasses. Special trifocal lenses designed with a broad middle-distance area are available for VDT workers. But whatever you do, don't let sore eyes make you dependent on over-the-counter eye-whitening drops. These drops clear up bloodshot eyes by constricting the blood vessels in the whites of the eye and have no curative powers. Your eyes may look better, but they won't feel better. But if your problem is irritation caused by dry eyes, imitation-tears eye drops may provide temporary relief.

NEARSIGHTEDNESS

Myopia, or nearsightedness, affects about 30 percent of all Americans and is the most common problem of aging eyes in those under 45. A study conducted by the National Society to Prevent Blindness found that, in a given year, one-third of all people seeking help for nearsightedness were between the ages of 25 and 44.

Nearsighted people have trouble seeing distant objects because the visual image transmitted back into their eye comes to a focus in front of the retina, not on it. Until recently, scientists believed that myopia was an inherited condition caused by the eyeball being too deep from front to back. Now some researchers suggest that it may be a learned cultural habit. Because we live in a society that prizes literacy and other close-up skills, they say, we repeatedly focus on near objects, training our eyes and brains to consider faraway objects as less important.

Whatever the cause, myopia is easily correctable in almost all cases. Glasses or contact lenses solve the problem by changing light refraction so that the image comes into focus on the retina. For those who want clear vision without glasses or contacts, there is a controversial surgical technique called radial keratotomy that slices the cornea, changing its shape and thus the light refraction patterns. But the precise amount of correction is difficult to predict, and there are questions about the operation's permanence.

PRESBYOPIA

Reading glasses rank with gray hair and crow's-feet as early visible signs of aging. Nearly everyone over 40 begins to have trouble focusing on fine print. The problem is called presbyopia (*presby* is Greek for "old"), a normal degenerative change caused by a loss of the lens' ability to change shape. Until mid-life, muscles surrounding the lens are able to to flatten it or make it rounder to focus on distant or near objects. This system works well as long as the lens itself is flexible. But as time passes, its inner cells die and lose their elasticity, making the lens stiff. At birth, your lens is like pliable plastic; by age 50 it is nearly glasslike.

Blurry print is the first sign of presbyopia. You hold the newspaper farther and farther away from your eyes until you run out of arm. Then you get an eye exam. Reading glasses easily solve the problem. For those with existing vision problems, bifocals—now made without the telltale line separating close and distant corrective lenses—might be the answer. Contact lenses come in bifocal prescriptions as well. A few doctors believe that fine-print, low-light visual exercises, if performed religiously, can improve the lens' focusing ability. But most say corrective lenses are the only solution.

CATARACTS

A much more serious—but also, happily, correctable—problem of the aging eye is the formation of cataracts, a clouding or yellowing of the normally transparent lens. Cataracts eventually block light from entering the eye, causing dim or blurry vision and, according to National Society to Prevent Blindness statistics, affecting, to some degree, three out of four 60-year-olds.

The French impressionist painter Claude Monet provides a vivid illustration of what cataracts can do to your sight. He was in his late 60s when his eyesight and his paintings changed dramatically. Individual objects ceased to exist. The canvases became swirls of muddy color. But for Monet and millions of other less famous cataract sufferers, cloudiness in the lens may begin decades before any change in vision is evident.

The traditional explanation for slow-growing cataracts is that fibers in the lens continue to form throughout our lives, with new ones on the periphery compressing the older ones in toward the center. As the years go by, the older fibers become so compressed and densely packed that the lens turns milky. Because the process is so gradual, most people don't notice any visual impairment until their 60s.

But new evidence suggests that not all cataracts are an inevitable consequence of aging. As many as 25 percent of all cataracts may form because of exposure to the sun—and may be preventable. Donald Pitts, a professor of environmental optometry at the University of Houston who has been studying cataracts for more than 20 years, believes he has established an undeniable link between excessive exposure to ultraviolet light and the clouding of the lens of the eye. A growing body of research from around the world corroborates his findings.

If he's right, wearing sunglasses now may save you from undergoing eye surgery decades later. But not just any sunglasses. The lenses, which must be ultraviolet-absorbing, are generally not found in inexpensive, over-the-counter sunglasses. Experts caution that the darkness of the lens is not an accurate indicator of its protective capabilities. For ultraviolet-blocking lenses, see your ophthalmologist or optometrist.

If the lens of the eye becomes so opaque that it interferes with sight, the only option is surgically removing the lens. In Monet's day, the operation was painful, the recuperative period lengthy and the results a matter of chance. Today, eye surgeons are removing cloudy lenses and replacing them, inside the eye, with high-tech plastic lenses that provide clearer vision immediately after surgery.

GLAUCOMA

It's a sneaky disease. You notice few symptoms. By the time you realize something is wrong, you've already suffered irreparable damage. Glaucoma affects two million people, strikes one person out of 50 over age 35 and is three times more prevalent among women and blacks than the general population. After age 40, it is a leading cause of blindness.

WOMEN'S EYES

No one knows why, but it seems women tend to see slightly less clearly than men. In a National Health Survey that tested men and women from ages four to 74 (with corrective lenses if they wore them), 75 percent of the men but only 70 percent of the women tested at least 20/20. Also for reasons yet unknown, women are three times more likely than men to suffer from chronic glaucoma.

Hormones are linked to some problems. An increased risk of blood clots in the back of the eye (and elsewhere) is associated with pregnancy and certain oral contraceptives. Difficulties wearing hard contact lenses increase when women are pregnant or on the Pill because certain female hormones seem to soften the cornea slightly.

Cosmetics may also cause trouble. When bits of

mascara flake off and become lodged between the eyelid and eye, irritation can develop. Some women have strong allergic reactions to the fragrances and preservatives in eye cosmetics. Others may suffer from eye infections when their makeup becomes a breeding ground for bacteria picked up from the skin and lashes.

The problem is one of balance. The eye continually produces a clear fluid that bathes the lens, carries nutrients to inner structures and then drains away into the bloodstream. When all goes well, fluid produced equals fluid drained, and the pressure within the eye remains constant. But if drainage channels become blocked, fluid builds up and creates pressure.

The eye itself can withstand this, but the optic nerve cannot. In the most common form of glaucoma, the pressure gradually destroys the fibers of the nerve, beginning with those that communicate peripheral vision signals to the brain.

Not surprisingly, one indication of glaucoma is impaired side vision. Periodic blurring or hazing, trouble adjusting to a darkened room, difficulty focusing on close work and rainbow halos around lights at night are also telltale signs. But these symptoms appear so gradually and painlessly that most people don't notice them until the disease is well on its way, and parts of the optic nerve are already destroyed. As yet, medical science has not discovered a way to repair the damage.

That's why early diagnosis and treatment is so vital. The test for the disease is simple and painless and should be part of your regularly scheduled eye exam. Treatment during its early stages can arrest glaucoma and minimize vision loss. Eye drops, long a mainstay of medical treatment, can reduce pressure in the eye by improving drainage of fluid or decreasing its rate of production. Some of the same kind of medication is available in pill form. Both laser surgery and ultrasound treatments can create new drainage channels for excess fluid. The newest treatment, dubbed a "glaucoma eyelift," concentrates on the meshwork inside the front of the eye that normally soaks up eye fluid. This spongy ring, like skin, stretches out over time and loses its ability to absorb. A laser beam creates a hundred microscopic burns in the meshwork, and as the wounds heal, the spongy ring shrinks taut and regains its function.

SENILE MACULAR DEGENERATION

Senile Macular Degeneration (SMD) has nothing to do with senility, but it is age-related. Although anyone can suffer this kind of visual impairment—and 10 million Americans do—SMD tends to strike people in their 50s and 60s. In fact, it is the leading cause of blindness and severe vision loss in retirement-age people. Why concern yourself with it now? Because early detection may help save your sight.

With SMD, blood vessels in the layer behind the retina grow forward and leak fluid or blood under the macula, a tiny region of the retina responsible for central vision. As the cells of the macula are destroyed, all but peripheral vision becomes increasingly distorted. Unfortunately the cause is unknown, and the effects irreversible.

Scientists at the National Eye Institute have recently developed a technique that is helping to save the sight of six to eight percent of SMD sufferers. Surgeons using lasers focus a beam of light to seal up the blood vessels before continued leakage causes major loss. The treatment doesn't cure SMD, but it does stop further deterioration. The earlier the diagnosis and treatment, the more sight can be saved. Toward that end, experts recommend regular eye exams and a simple, at-home eye test known as the Minnesota Adult Home Eye Screening Test.

PREVENTIVE EYE CARE

High-tech treatments and advanced lens technology now mean that most of us can continue to see well, even as our eyes age and change. But there's one catch: The key to success in most treatments is early detection. And ophthalmologists say that most adults have infrequent eye exams, seeking care only after they notice vision loss. More often than not, treatment is possible, but the loss already suffered is irreversible.

Experts differ on how frequently we ought to have our eyes examined. Some say every two years between 20 and 45 and annually thereafter. Others say annual exams ought to begin at 40 or even 35. Most stress the need for regular glaucoma testing after age 40.

WHO ARE THE SPECIALISTS?

Where do you go when you need eye surgery, a complete eye exam, a vision test, new glasses? Eye care professionals have different training, qualifications and expertise, and in the past there's been some rivalry between the professions. These definitions will help you choose the right specialist:

- *Ophthalmologists* are fully trained physicians (M.D.s) with a specialty in eye-related disorders. Like all medical doctors, they go through four years of medical school, an internship and a hospital residency before they begin in private practice. Ophthalmologists conduct complete eye exams and diagnose, treat and prescribe drugs for eye diseases. They also give vision exams and prescribe glasses or contacts. Some but not all ophthalmologists are eye surgeons who perform various in-office and hospital procedures.
- *Optometrists* examine, measure and treat those visual faults that can be corrected with eyeglasses or contact lenses. They attend a four-year school of optometry after college, where they become specialists in the anatomy of the eye and the properties of corrective lenses. Although optometrists carry the title "doctor of optometry" (O.D.), they are not medical doctors, cannot perform surgery and, in most states, cannot prescribe drugs. Visual-acuity tests and contact-lens fitting are their specialties.
- *Opticians* make and sell glasses and contacts. Depending on state requirements, they have been trained for one to two years in lens technology. No college degree is required, but there are certification and licensing requirements for those who want to become members of the Opticians Association of America.

What else can you do to help protect your sight? Here are ten suggestions from the experts:

1.   Never look directly into the sun or ultraviolet lamps. Wear polarized, mirrored or ultraviolet-absorbing lenses, especially when you're on the water, at the beach or on the ski slopes.
2.   Get enough sleep.
3.   Don't rely on fluorescent overhead lights when you're doing detail work or close reading. Use a tabletop lamp with regular bulb.
4.   While doing close work at the computer or elsewhere, give your eyes frequent rests. At least once every two hours, close them for a few minutes, then focus on a faraway object.
5.   Be an informed and careful consumer: Ask your doctor if any medications you take can cause eye complications.

MEDICINES AND DRUGS THAT CAN HURT YOUR EYES

Sudden eye pain or an abrupt change in vision may be the result of a drug you're taking for an unrelated problem. Most medications have some side effects for some people some of the time. These medicines and drugs can cause eye problems.

- *Nonprescription cold remedies and antihistamines* containing belladonna alkaloids (powerful nerve-blocking chemicals) occasionally cause a particularly severe and damaging form of glaucoma. If you're a frequent pill popper, you should have your eye pressure checked.
- *Oral contraceptives* have been implicated in severe damage to the blood vessels of the retina. Although this effect is uncommon, women on the Pill should inform heir ophthalmologists.
- *Anti-inflammatory drugs* like cortisone, when used for prolonged periods, may lead to chronic glaucoma, cataracts or damaged eye muscles. If you're on this therapy and experience blurred or dimmed vision, loss of peripheral vision, halos around objects of light or severe headaches, see your ophthalmologist.

- *Certain antibiotics* (chloramphenicol), *migraine headache medications* (ergotamine compounds) *and tubercular drugs* (isoniazid and ethambutol) have been implicated in dangerous swelling of the optic nerve. Make sure your ophthalmologist knows you are taking these drugs.
- *Certain anti-malarial medications* (chloroquine hydrochloride, atabrine) can destroy retinal tissue and cause irreversible loss of central vision. Chloroquine is also used to treat lupus, a family of skin diseases.
- *Alcohol*—the most common drug in America—can, when chronically abused, lead to progressive dimness of vision that may result in legal blindness. Current research suggests that the poor nutrition often accompanying alcohol abuse may be the real culprit.

---

6. Use safety goggles whenever you work with tools that can scatter debris like saws, drills, chisels and electric clippers.
7. Protect yourself at play. Wear heavy-duty polycarbonate goggles when playing racquet sports. When you swim, wear goggles.
8. Handle chemicals cautiously. Wear goggles when spraying herbicides or pesticides in the garden. Use household cleaning solutions with care.
9. If you get a foreign object or harmful substance in your eye, don't rub it. In most cases, flushing the eye with water is the best remedy. Check the instructions on the substance you were using.
10. Don't ignore any eye symptoms. Sudden eye pain, severe sensitivity to light, distortion, blurriness, blind spots and halos around bright lights can all be signs of serious eye problems. When you notice these symptoms, see your doctor.

EYES AND NUTRITION

Will eating carrots improve your eyesight? Is it possible to slow or stop age-related eye damage by including certain foods in your diet? Few experts would argue that a vital requirement for healthy eyes is a healthy body, but research on most individual vitamins and minerals is inconclusive. Here's a rundown on current scientific findings:

- *Vitamin A.* The link between vitamin A and night blindness is well established. The cells lining the retina need vitamin A to form a light-sensitive pigment that enables us to see in dim light. Orange, yellow and dark green vegetables, milk and eggs are the best food sources.
- *Zinc.* More recently, scientists have discovered that zinc is important in converting vitamin A to its active, usable form. A study at Johns Hopkins Hospital and the University of Maryland School of Medicine concluded that both zinc and vitamin A are key ingredients in the chemistry of night vision. Whole-grain products, wheat bran and wheat germ, seafood and meat are the best food sources.
- *Vitamin C.* Studies show that a healthy eye lens is rich in vitamin C while a diseased one contains little. In Australia, a national health study involving more than 100,000 people found evidence that vitamin C inhibited clouding of the lens caused by exposure to ultraviolet light. But how much vitamin C, when and for whom are all questions still to be answered. There's also some scientific support for vitamin C as a glaucoma treatment. Fresh fruits and vegetables are the best food sources.
- *Vitamin E.* Hailed by some as a major "anti-aging" nutrient, vitamin E is currently being studied by National Eye Institute researchers. They suspect that the retina is highly susceptible to oxidation and that vitamin E, a powerful antioxidant, can protect it from age-related degeneration. But so far, their tests have been limited to laboratory animals. Whole-grain cereals, eggs, vegetable oils, enriched flour and leafy greens are the best food sources.
- *Folic acid.* Johns Hopkins Hospital researchers are studying the possibility that folic acid or some other unknown vitamin from green and yellow vegetables may be essential to normal vision and healthy optic-nerve function. Green and yellow vegetables are the best food sources.

If there is a magic dietary formula that will keep your eyes—and the rest of you—from aging, medical science has yet to discover it. In the meantime, it's wise to shy away from faddish megadosing, which can sometimes do more harm than good. Overdoses of vitamin A, for example, can cause inflammation of the optic nerve and severe, often irreversible loss of vision. The best nutritional plan is still a balanced diet rich in fresh, unprocessed foods and easy on caffeinated and alcoholic drinks.

8
Hearing

Imagine an audio system that amplifies sound 18,000 percent, a system so sensitive that it can pick up a vibration less than the diameter of a hydrogen molecule yet so sturdy that a sound 10 million million times louder will not damage its mechanisms. Now couple this sound system with an advanced gyroscope, miniaturize the entire package to one cubic inch and guarantee its parts for more than 60 years.

Sounds like an engineer's dream? It is. It's the human ear.

One of our major sensory links to the outside world, the ear brings us sounds—from the soft hiss of rain to the incessant roar of traffic—that link us to our environment. Steadfastly indiscriminate, it alerts us to everything from chainsaws to Tchaikovsky.

The fanciful swirl of skin and cartilage most of us think of as the ear is merely a funnel that scoops up sound waves and bounces them down an inch-long canal to the eardrum. When sound waves hit this thin, white membrane, it reverberates, transmitting these vibrations through a chain of three tiny bones in the middle ear. The last of these bones rests against a fluid-filled snail-shaped coil in the inner ear. Vibrations set the fluid moving, and exquisitely sensitive hairs in the coil react biochemically, sending "sound" messages through a major nerve to the brain.

When all its finely tuned parts work in concert, the human ear can pick up sounds as soft as a baby's breathing down the hall and as loud as a thunderclap overhead. Undamaged by age, noise or disease, the human ear can hear frequencies higher than a "silent" dog whistle and lower than the bass note on a piano. But the mechanisms of the ear, like all our body parts, do show the effects of time.

HEARING LOSS

Whether due to the natural aging process or the cumulative ravages of living in a noisy world, our hearing becomes less acute as we grow older. The downside is that hearing loss in the higher frequencies begins soon after birth and continues throughout life. The consolation is that most people who suffer auditory problems can improve their hearing.

NEWBORNS: Can hear as high as 20,000 hertz ("inaudible" anti-theft devices in stores)
AGE 25:   Trouble hearing above 16,000 hertz (a cricket's chirp)
AGE 45:   Trouble hearing above 12,000 hertz (some bird songs)
AGE 60:   Trouble hearing above 10,000 hertz (some bird songs)
AGE 80:   Trouble hearing above 6,000 hertz (whistling teapot)

WHAT HAPPENS TO EARS AS WE AGE?

Changes in the ear are slow, progressive and painless. They begin at birth—we never hear as well as we do when we're newborns—and continue unabated throughout our lives. In fact, one researcher estimates that if we lived to be 140, we'd all be deaf. Some age-related changes are serious and do affect our hearing. Others are entirely innocuous, even (if we can maintain our sense of humor) somewhat amusing:

- Ears get bigger. Of course we're all born with individually crafted and differently sized outer ears, but if you've noticed that older people seem to have larger lobes and grander swirls, your eyes are not deceiving you. It's one of nature's harmless jokes that the outer ear grows slowly and continuously throughout life. The lobe elongates as gravity pulls it downward.
- Hairs grow in the outer ear and ear canal. This unwelcome age-related occurrence is nothing more than an aesthetic problem. Probably kicked off by some hormonal sequence, it generally affects men rather than women.
- Earwax is produced more abundantly. An annoying but necessary secretion produced by the cells of the outer ear, earwax normally works its way outward and can be easily removed with a washcloth. Some people naturally produce more earwax than others, regardless of age. But in general, older people tend to produce more than younger. This can become more than mere annoyance if the wax collects and hardens in the ear canal, blocking the passage of sound waves. The result is temporary hearing impairment.
- The ultrasensitive hairs in the fluid-filled coil of the inner ear begin to break down. Scientists debate how much of this degeneration is a consequence of natural aging and how much is the price we pay for living in a noisy world, but the result is the same: permanent, irreversible hearing loss. Because the hairs tuned to the highest frequencies are most affected, hearing loss occurs first in the upper ranges. Men, perhaps because they have traditionally been exposed to noisier work environments, have tended to suffer more hearing loss than women.
- The small arteries in the inner ear, like the arteries throughout the body, show the effects of age. Because they decrease in size and their walls thicken, they are able to carry less nourishment to inner ear structures.

Most experts believe that at least some hearing loss is inevitable as we grow older. And most of the statistics they cite are not encouraging: Researchers at the National Institutes of Health estimate that close to half those older than 50 have some kind of impairment detectable on standard hearing tests. Roughly 10 percent, they say, have an obvious hearing handicap. Other experts calculate that 18 million people—one out of 13 Americans—suffer some degree of hearing loss. But there is one encouraging statistic: Professionals believe that 90 percent of people with auditory problems can improve their hearing through medical treatment, surgery or artificial devices.

Because hearing loss is slow, painless and generally limited to high frequencies, most people in their 20s, 30s and 40s aren't even aware that their hearing is diminishing. But eventually, loss in the high frequencies can erode the clarity and understandability of conversation.

TWO KINDS OF HEARING LOSS

Doctors talk about two kinds of hearing loss: *conductive* and *sensory-neural*. Conductive loss, caused by something blocking the sound as it travels through the outer and middle ear, reduces sensitivity to all sound regardless of frequency. It is the less serious and more treatable of the two kinds of loss.

Some conductive loss is not age-related. Middle-ear infections and diseases, which may occur more frequently in childhood and young adulthood, can cause conductive loss. So can punctured eardrums. Age plays a part when excessive wax build-up impacts within the ear canal and interferes with sound waves traveling toward the eardrum. Wax plugs may even press against the eardrum, preventing it from vibrating. The problem is more common than you may think. One study found that 30 percent of people who came in for auditory exams complaining of hearing loss suffered only from impacted wax.

Fortunately, virtually all conductive disorders can be medically or surgically treated and cured. Doctors can quickly and painlessly remove earwax build-up by softening it with oil and flushing it from the ear canal with a stream of water. Antibiotics can effectively fight middle-ear infections. Delicate but usually successful surgery can repair certain disease-caused middle-ear problems.

Of greater concern is sensory-neural loss—sometimes known as "nerve deafness"—because it involves permanent, often incurable impairment. Here the problem lies in the inner ear with the fragile hairs inside the snail-shaped coil or with the auditory nerve itself. In some cases congenital disorders, metabolic disturbances, allergies, syphilis or auditory nerve tumors can cause nerve deafness. But most sensory-neural loss can be traced to two interconnected causes: normal attrition of hair cells within the inner ear coil and damage to these cells caused by noise pollution. Once damaged, the cells cannot regenerate, and the frequencies they were attuned to are no longer audible.

PRESBYCUSIS

Age-related loss of hearing is called presbycusis (from the Greek "presby" meaning old and "cusis" meaning ear). It's really a catchall term for a variety of sensory-neural problems caused by what researchers consider normal deterioration of the auditory system. Although termed an older person's disease, it actually begins early in life when inner-ear hair cells begin to die. Hearing loss—at first slight and un-noticeable—accumulates slowly over many years. Only after loss reaches a certain break point, usually in the 60s or beyond, do we realize anything has happened.

High-frequency hearing is most affected, but presbycusis sufferers may also experience a loss of sensitivity to all sound or the ability to distinguish certain words in speech. Typically, their first reaction is that others are suddenly speaking softly or indistinctly. It often doesn't occur to them, especially if they're otherwise healthy and active, that their own hearing is diminishing.

Unlike some other hearing impairments, presbycusis is permanent—and, as yet, incurable. But that doesn't mean all sufferers must resign themselves to the sounds of silence. Hearing aids, including high-tech masterpieces computer-designed to fit the individual, are helping to compensate for aging nerve cells. While the devices do not cure the problem, they do help the vast majority of presbycusis victims hear better.

What can you do to prevent presbycusis? Nothing, say many specialists. Deteriorating hair cells in the inner ear's spiral coil are a natural consequence of aging, they say, and there's no way to stop the process. Others disagree. They contend that much of the damage now attributed to age is really caused by living in a noisy world. Avoid noise and you avoid hearing loss, they say.

NOISE

Somewhere near the border of Sudan and Ethiopia lives a tribe called the Mabaans. Considered "primitive" by anthropologists, they are in at least two ways more civilized than we are: They don't shout at each other, and they don't fire guns. Their lives include no clanking machinery. Even their music, which they play softly and without drums, is restful. It was into this hushed world that a New York City audiologist intruded some years ago.

After testing the hearing of 500 tribesman, the audiologist and his research team discovered something extraordinary: There was virtually no difference in the hearing of 30-year-olds and 70-year-olds. Almost every tribesman tested could hear a soft murmur across a clearing the size of a football field. Where was evidence of the "natural" aging process that was supposed to rob older ears of their acuity?

Some took the Mabaan study to mean that the clatter of civilized life, not age, causes progressive hearing loss. Others criticized the study's methods, pointed to lack of corroborating evidence and stuck to their age thesis. But regardless of the ongoing debate, everyone agrees that noise itself damages hearing.

As many as 25 million Americans are regularly exposed to noise loud and continuous enough to cause permanent hearing loss. Considered the most widespread occupational hazard, excessive noise is almost as much a part of home and recreational environments as it is of the workplace.

Prolonged exposure to intense noise, says University of California researcher A.J. Hudspeth, "chops, dices and otherwise hacks apart" the hair cells designed to respond to much softer sounds. And prolonged exposure is a fact of life for many urbanites. According to the President's Council on Environmental Quality, at least 13.5 million Americans are regularly to exposed traffic noise of 75 decibels or more—a level considered sufficient to risk permanent hearing damage. In New York City, rail rapid-transit noise at 85 to 100 decibels assaults the ears of an estimated half-million people every day. In California, a research team found that thousands of children who attend schools along the Los Angeles International air corridor are subjected to blasts of 95 decibels every 2.5 minutes.

And then there's the noise we purposefully inflict on ourselves. Music inside concert halls and clubs has been clocked at 120 decibels. At that level, according to Occupational Safety and Health Administration (OSHA) standards, just 10 minutes of exposure can cause permanent hearing damage. Even worse for our ears than the roar of live rock (or, for that matter, symphonic) concerts are headphones and portable earphone listening systems. Very efficient stereo and headphone sets are capable of delivering more than 135 decibels with peak sounds in the 150-decibel range, about what you'd experience if you rode inside a jet engine at take-off. And headphones or earphones deliver a direct blast. Sound waves travel only an inch before they hit

THE HAZARDS OF A NOISY WORLD

Just how noisy a world do you live in? When does noise cease to be merely annoying and start to be hazardous to your hearing? This is what the experts say:

Noise	Sound level (decibels)	Dangerous time exposure
Rustle of leaf	10	
Library, quiet whisper	30	
Quiet office or home	40	
Light auto traffic at a distance	50	
Conversation	60	Critical level begins
Busy traffic, noisy restaurant	70	Damage possible after 8 hrs.
Subway, factory noise, urban apartment	80	Damage possible in less than 8 hrs.
Truck traffic, shop tools, lawnmower	90	Damage possible in 2 hrs.
Jackhammer, chainsaw, garbage truck	100	Immediate danger
Rock concert (in front of speakers)	120	Any exposure is dangerous
Jet plane, gunshot, air raid siren	140	

the eardrum. Nothing helps buffer or absorb the sound like furniture, drapes or carpet.

Researchers now say they're uncovering "an awesome trend" toward loss of high-frequency hearing among today's young adults. Even more disturbing, recent audiological surveys are finding that the entire body reacts to noise as stress. California scientists discovered that children exposed to overhead aircraft noise throughout the day had significantly higher blood pressure and greater difficulty solving problems and puzzles than their peers in quieter classrooms. Not only that, but some research suggests that the body doesn't seem to adapt to noise even though the mind may. Although you can intellectually tune out noise, your body continues to react to it as stress.

Millions of Americans face the risk of both hearing impairment and stress-related problems from hypertension to memory loss because of their work environments. OSHA estimates that half the nation's production workers are exposed to workplace noise of 80 decibels or higher. But it's not just millworkers or jackhammer operators whose jobs may be hazardous to their health. White-collar professionals like symphonic musicians and dentists may also be at risk. OSHA does set maximum noise-level standards to protect workers. But according to researchers at the National Institute of Occupational Safety and Health, 29 percent of workers exposed to no more that the federal standard will suffer permanent hearing loss.

YOUR JOB AND YOUR HEARING

As many as one in ten Americans are exposed to noise loud enough and long enough to cause permanent hearing loss. The clatter of urban life—from freeway traffic to boom boxes—accounts for some of this exposure. The rest occurs in the workplace.

According to the Environmental Protection Agency, 75 decibels is the maximum sound level most adults can be exposed to for eight hours a day throughout a 40-year career without risking hearing loss.

People who work in the following jobs are often exposed to noise levels at or above 75 decibels:

- airline ground crews
- dental hygienists
- dentists
- factory production workers (esp. textile and lumber mills)
- harbor and dock workers
- heavy-machine operators
- meat cutters
- military personnel (gun and artillery fire)
- musicians and their crews (from symphonic to rock)

- race car drivers
- railroad workers
- subway operators
- truck and bus drivers

What can you do to protect yourself from excessive noise?

- Use an ear-protection device whenever your environment is noisy—at work, at home (remember power tools and lawnmowers) or at play (guns, speedboats). You can buy three basic types of protection: earplugs, which fit into the ear canal; canal caps, which cover the entrance to the ear canal; and earmuffs, which fit over and around the ears. Earmuffs appear to block the most sound. Experts also recommend delayed-recovery foam earplugs that compress in your fingers and expand for a custom fit in your ears.
- If you listen to music with earphones or a portable earplug system, turn the volume down. Remember that music played at the same volume on your stereo doesn't blast directly into your ear canal. How loud is too loud? Audiologists say that if you can't converse with the person next to you, the volume is too high.
- If you attend live concerts, be they Springsteen or Sibelius, don't position yourself near any loudspeakers.
- If you live on a noisy street, consider double-paned windows or thick drapes to help muffle the din.

TINNITUS

One sign that we've exposed our ears to more than they can handle is ringing in the ears or tinnitus. The sound—anything from a soft hiss to a wild screech—may last only a few minutes. For the unlucky ones, tinnitus becomes a fact of daily life. Our ear, says the head of the Kresge Hearing Research Laboratory in Portland, Oregon, "is too sensitive for its own good."

More than 35 million Americans suffer from tinnitus to some degree, according to a National Institutes of Health survey. For some, tinnitus is a mild annoyance; for others, the buzzing and ringing can be severe enough to disrupt normal activities. The noise may be present in one or both ears, may be different in each ear and may change in intensity or pitch during the day. Sounds can come and go at random.

Constant or long-term exposure to loud noise is the major villain, but tinnitus has other causes as well. Viral infections, head injuries and impacted earwax are all contributors. So is emotional stress or excessive amounts of aspirin, alcohol or tobacco.

What should you do if you hear sounds your companions don't? First, see your physician or an ear specialist. Your problem may be impacted wax, an ear infection or some other treatable condition. Next, evaluate the extent of your vices and, if necessary, cut alcohol, caffeine and nicotine consumption. If the problem persists, you might consider hypnosis, acupuncture or biofeedback. These unconventional methods have proved successful for some long-time sufferers. At the Ear Research Institute in Los Angeles, 79 percent of patients with severe and unrelenting tinnitus found varying degrees of relief after a dozen one-hour biofeedback sessions. Your physician may have suggestions concerning drug therapy or surgical treatment. If all else fails, you may want to consider a tinnitus masker, a device that looks like a hearing aid but actually produces its own sound. The noise, which sounds like the hum of an air conditioner, smothers the inner noises of tinnitus. Sufferers apparently find the masker's sound more acceptable.

EAR CARE

Caring for and protecting ears can mean more years of sharper hearing. In addition to avoiding excessive noise or shielding your ears from its worst effects, here's what you can do to keep your ears healthy:

- Clean only the outer ear. Earwax normally works itself out of the ear canal to where you can reach it with an washcloth. If you use a cotton swab or insert anything in your ear canal to try to remove the wax, you will only succeed in pushing it down toward the eardrum and impacting it. If you produce excessive earwax, have your doctor clean your ears for you.
- To prevent swimmer's ear—an infection caused by trapped water in the ear canal—shake, tilt and tap your head if you feel water in your ears. If this doesn't do the trick, try a dropperful of alcohol, alcohol-vinegar mix or over-the-counter swimmer's ear eardrops. Remember

that swimmers are not the only ones at risk. Anyone who takes a shower or bath can get water trapped in the ear. If you have any perforations in your eardrum, audiologists caution you not to use drops.

- When traveling by air, prevent discomfort by staying awake while taking off and landing, and swallowing, yawning or chewing gum to equalize air pressure between the outer and middle ear. Avoid alcohol before and during the flight. If you have a cold, use a nasal-decongestant spray before takeoff.
- Protect your ears from the elements. Wear a hat to prevent frostbite. Apply sunscreen to prevent sunburn.
- Be an aware consumer of medications. Certain drugs are known to damage hearing either temporarily or permanently. Researchers are discovering that some of these drugs multiply the damaging effect of

---

DRUGS THAT CAN CAUSE HEARING PROBLEMS

Some drugs are known to cause permanent hearing loss. Others temporarily affect hearing or cause related problems. Be aware that the following substances may damage your hearing:

- *Alcohol*, when consistently abused, can lead to hearing loss.
- *Caffeine*, in excessive amounts, can cause ringing in the ear (tinnitus).
- *Aspirin*, in large quantities (20 tablets daily), can cause temporary hearing loss.
- *Antibiotics* like streptomycin and neomycin are known to damage parts of the ear and cause permanent hearing loss.
- Certain powerful *loop diuretics* can temporarily impair hearing.
- Certain *local anesthetics* like lidocaine and procaine hydrochloride can cause temporary hearing loss.
- Certain *cancer-treatment* drugs can cause permanent damage to the ears.

---

noise. Quiz your physician about the potential side effects of all medications.

Yet another way to be kind to your ears is to have them examined or tested every few years after age 40. The two most common tests performed in hearing clinics are the pure-tone hearing test, which can determine the frequencies of hearing loss; and impedance audiometry, which measures how well the structures within the middle ear respond to sound waves.

SORTING OUT THE SPECIALISTS

Who should you see if you have an ear infection or are suffering from ringing in the ears? Who can evaluate your hearing? Who do you consult about hearing aids? Here's a guide to the specialists:

- *Otolaryngologists*—you know them as "ear, nose and throat doctors"—are M.D.s who specialize in diagnosing and treating diseases affecting these interconnected systems. They may also be plastic and reconstructive surgeons.
- *Otologists* are medical doctors who specialize in diagnosis and medical and surgical treatment of ear diseases.
- *Audiologists* are university-trained specialists with M.S. or Ph.D degrees) who administer hearing tests, evaluate the nature of hearing loss and prescribe and fit hearing aids. They also work with the hearing-impaired on lip reading, sign language and other rehabilitative efforts.
- *Hearing-aid dealers* are sales personnel who need have no special training. They help fit and dispense hearing aids.

HEARING AND NUTRITION

What we eat affects all parts of our bodies, and our ears are no exception. In addition to common-sense eating (a diet high in fresh, unprocessed foods and low in fat and refined sugar) and limited caffeine and alcohol consumption, some holistically oriented doctors and audiologists consider the following to be particularly important:

- **Sodium and potassium**. These two minerals constitute the chief ingredients of the fluid in the inner ear. When they're not in balance—some say this is common in our nation of salt-lovers—our hearing may suffer. To help regain and maintain the balance, cut down on salt and eat potassium-rich foods like salmon, chicken and bananas.
- **B vitamins**. They contribute to a healthy nervous system and help our bodies deal with stress. Vitamin B6 apparently helps prevent sodium retention. Leafy green vegetables, whole grains, eggs and liver are rich sources.
- **Vitamin A**. There's evidence that the hair cells within the inner ear's spiral coil are dependent on vitamin A. Orange, yellow and dark green vegetables, milk and eggs are good sources.

HIGH-TECH HEARING

The science of audiology has come a long way since ear trumpets and clumsy contraptions. If age, noise or disease does result in hearing problems that affect daily life, neither your hearing nor vanity need suffer. The vast majority of hearing aids fit inconspicuously in the ear or behind it. And microcomputers are helping scientists design aids to precisely fit individual requirements. It is now possible to overcome such problems as background noise with these new high-tech devices.

For those who have particular trouble hearing high-frequency sound or soft voices, Stanford Medical Center researchers have developed the "earesonator." A small, clear plastic bubble that fits in the outer ear, it changes the shape of the ear's swirl, lowering the frequency of high sounds and making them more audible.

The news for those with severe hearing problems is promising. The FDA recently approved an "electronic ear" system that includes a permanent implant in the inner ear, a tiny microphone and an above-ear transmitter. University of Florida researchers are experimenting with artificial middle-ear bones. At North Carolina's Triangle Research Institute, researchers are testing a device called an "autocuer." Designed for the deaf, it includes a microphone and microcomputer which convert speech into electronic symbols that appear on a magnified display built into a pair of eyeglasses.

9

Taste and Smell

Nature has outfitted us with a detection system for every need: sight for light energy, hearing for the vibrating air molecules we call sound, touch for temperature and pressure changes. Smell and taste are designed to detect and discriminate among chemicals. Devoting two senses to the job underlines its importance in our lives.

Sure, you may be thinking, it's nice to sniff a rose or savor a steak, but the loss of one or the other of these "secondary" senses wouldn't be a tragedy, right?

Wrong. Ask one of the millions of older people who suffer some degree of diminished smell and taste. They enjoy life less. Food loses its appeal, and in some cases malnutrition becomes a problem. The smell of a gas leak or the smoke from a house fire can go undetected, resulting in disaster.

After decades of concentrating on sight and hearing, scientists are only now beginning to pay much attention to smell and taste. And, although the research is still scant, early findings indicate that these senses may be important in much more than relishing a meal. The sense of smell, for example, appears to play a role in family bonding, memory function and hormonal response. This early research also indicates that both the senses diminish as we age.

SMELL

We use our sense of smell to detect the small molecules emitted by virtually every animal and plant — and many nonliving substances — that we call odors. Tracking down and analyzing these airborne chemicals is vital for most animals' hunting, defense and, in many cases, mating.

Humans may have lost much of that old-time need for the sense of smell, but the machinery is still intact. It all starts in the nose—but not that fleshy knob protruding from your face. The sense organ itself lies deeper and higher in the head, in a cavity between the roof of the mouth and the bones enclosing the brain. The ceiling of this space is coated with a dense layer of millions of receptor cells—as many or more receptors than in the eye—each crowned with a thatch of hairlike cilia.

On the surface of these cilia are specialized sites that bind odor molecules. When odor meets cilia, it triggers a nerve impulse. A sniff of a complex odor, such as perfume, sets off a symphony of receptor signals.

What happens after that again underlines the importance of smell. Nerve impulses from other senses go through some sort of intermediate gateway before they reach the brain, but not so signals from the nose. The nerves carrying these impulses are wired directly into a primitive part of the brain called the olfactory bulb. Why this direct connection exists is a mystery researchers are seeking to solve. Some of them speculate it may have something to do with the links between odor and memory. Just the scent of someone's cologne, for example, can trigger a flood of feelings and memories.

Our sense of smell is also more acute than it has been given credit for. It was recently thought, for instance, that the human nose could only distinguish among 16 odors. Now we know that the limit is more in our brain than our olfactory apparatus. Because we've ignored our sense of smell, we haven't learned names for most odors. As a result, we may "know" that an odor is familiar, but can't name it. Researchers call it the "tip-of-the-nose phenomenon." Without being able to give a name to an odor, our brains can't use smell-related information as effectively—and we dismiss our sense of smell as unimportant.

But with proper training, the human nose can discriminate among hundreds, perhaps thousands of odors. Perfumers, with their well-trained noses, can detect the addition or loss of a single component in a complex scent. In laboratory tests, the human nose has been found more sensitive than the most sophisticated scientific equipment in detecting some compounds, picking up odors in concentrations of a few parts per billion.

TASTE

Another group of chemicals is important to us because we're considering eating them—and taste tells us something about their desirability. A much simpler system than the sense of smell, taste is set up to distinguish only four basic qualities: sweet, salty, sour and bitter. Everything else we taste, from chocolate to Chinese food, is courtesy of the sense of smell, which works in close harmony with taste. Test it: Hold your nose the next time you have a mouthful of something delicious.

Each of the thousands of taste buds scattered about the tongue (as well as the throat and soft palate) are composed of about 100 or so receptor cells. The receptors are mostly hidden, opening to the surface through a small taste bud pore. As a result, they work only when a chemical has been dissolved in liquid—most often your saliva—so it can get through the pore and make contact with hairlike structures that send off a nerve impulse.

Taste buds wear away and are replaced about every two weeks, making the system one of the most dynamic in the body. That's lucky, considering the tissue-damaging chemicals (like alcohol) and extreme temperatures to which we expose taste buds.

NORMAL AGING

A loss of acuity in both smell and taste is a fact of life for many older Americans.

The most current research from the Clinical Smell and Taste Research Center at the University of Pennsylvania shows that our ability to identify odors reaches a peak between ages 20 and 40, and then begins a long decline into old age. Investigators there found that more than 60 percent of the people they tested between 65 and 80 years old had "major impairment" of their sense of smell.

Why? Some researchers speculate that a gradual destruction of smell receptors is to blame. Others point to psychological factors associated with aging like the often self-fulfilling expectation that senses will dull. Still others are investigating the link between the diminishing senses of smell and taste and changes in hormonal levels. Because the decline in the ability to identify odors happens at the same rate as the decline in normal eyesight, there is some thought that problems with the nervous system in general may be to blame.

Odor receptors may be lost through illness, especially diseases that inflame the sinuses, and viral infections. Receptors can also be damaged through exposure to some chemicals, and scientists are currently looking at the effects of pollutants and chemicals in the workplace. Studies indicate that people who smoke tend to have more trouble indentifying odors than nonsmokers.

The effects of age on *detecting* odors, as opposed to identifying them, are just as confusing. Some researchers have found that sensitivity to odors goes down with age; others have found no age-related effect. In general, differences in overall health seem to affect sense of smell more than age.

Taste perception is a bit more clear-cut. Taste buds are concentrated on the small bumps (called papillae) that make the tongue's surface look rough. As children, we have about 250 buds per papillae. This number drops to about 90 by the time we're 80. The number of nerves leading out of the taste buds also declines with time, and the mouth produces less saliva to put flavors into solution.

As a result, the ability to taste sweet, sour and bitter things grows less acute as we grow older (although, interestingly, it appears the ability to taste salty things doesn't change much). Contrary to popular belief, we don't "burn out" our taste buds through years of eating spicey or peppery foods.

But it's still difficult to assign causes and effects. Taste perception and appetite can also be affected by psychological states, including depression, drug use and illness.

THE FUTURE

Scientists are currently pursuing several promising lines of research that may help our aging senses of smell and taste:

- *Learning to use what we've got.* Paying attention to the chemical senses—especially smell—can help us get more out of them as time goes on. Because of the importance of attaching a name to an odor, expanding smell and taste vocabularies is one way to increase enjoyment of the sense we've got. Winetasters and perfumers can distinguish fine gradations of taste and odor because they've trained themselves to do it—and because they've developed a vocabulary to work with. Think about what you're smelling, and work to find words to describe it.

THE BEER-DRINKERS VOCABULARY LIST

The more words you have to describe a taste or smell, the better able you are to appreciate it, remember it and discriminate it from others. Professionals who must use their noses know it's true. Take a tip from the following list of words, from a standardized system used by brewing chemists to describe the taste and odor of beers, and start thinking about flavors and smells in a new way.

Bitter	Salty
Sweet	Sour
Alkaline	Metallic
Astringent	Acidic
Yeasty	Malty
Grainy	Grassy
Nutty	Resinous
Hoppy	Floral
Fruity	Cooked vegetable
Sulfury	Oily
Burnt	Moldy
Leathery	Catty
Stale	Caramel

- *The hormonal link.* People's smell sensitivity changes on a monthly cycle, and women are more smell-sensitive than men—two facts that point to a link between sex hormones and the sense of smell. Hormones produced by the adrenal glands may also have an effect. When these hormones are eliminated by disease or surgery, the smell sensitivity of some patients is increased by as much as 100,000 times, making their noses sensitive enough to smell table sugar. Further research may provide some understanding of how to use the hormonal link to help stop the age-related decline. The link appears to work both ways: The sense of smell working with certain odors seems to affect hormonal responses. Groups of young women who live in close proximity over time, as in a dormitory, often synchronize their menstrual cycles. The triggers, evidence shows, are often-undetectable underarm odors.

- *Diet.* Adequate amounts of at least one dietary component are necessary to keep the chemical-detecting senses in good working order. Deficiencies of zinc can cause a loss of taste and alteration of smell. But simply replacing the zinc through a mineral supplement doesn't seem to help older people—suggesting a more complex mechanism at play. The key is eating a good, balanced diet, which should provide plenty of zinc.
- *Therapy.* While there's no magic pill to bring back the taste and smells of youth, at least one researcher is working on a method to make food taste better to older people suffering from a decline in the chemical-detecting senses. Susan Schiffman, a professor of medical psychology at Duke University, is studying the molecules that give foods their characteristic tastes. By reproducing these substances in crystal form in the lab, she has developed a group of flavor enhancers that contain no fat or salt. Among her crystals are the flavors of cream cheese and bacon.

Part IV
GETTING AROUND

10

Bones

Our bones outlast us. It's hard to imagine them changing with age because they seem rocklike and eternal, the last of us to turn to dust.

But change they do. The body dissolves and reforms our bones throughout life, remaking them faster than muscle, cartilage or any internal organs. It has to: Besides serving as a support system for the body, bones are used as a storehouse for minerals. When the body needs calcium, for instance, it gets it by breaking down the calcium salts that make bone hard and white. The salts are added back when there's a calcium surplus. The part of the process that involves breaking down bone is called resorption.

This constant give and take opens the door for gradual bone deterioration with age. And when the bones start to go, the body can fall prey to a variety of ills that can leave us hobbling and shuffling.

Unfortunately, most people don't think about deteriorating bones until it's too late—when bent, creaking frames and shrinking height start becoming evident in the 60s and 70s. But the seeds are planted much earlier.

Bone problems can start as soon as we stop growing. A youngster's bones grow and thicken because bone construction outpaces bone resorption. But in our mid-20s, the balance begins to shift. Buy our 40s, resorption can take the upper hand, weakening the body's skeletal system.

There are ways to fight weakening bones. In fact, nothing better illustrates the importance and effectiveness of preventive care than the skeleton and its associated muscles and ligaments. With regular exercise of the right sort—and proper diet—we can easily keep our bones in good shape throughout life.

OSTEOPOROSIS

Some amount of bone loss is normal with age. What is not normal is accelerated bone loss that can dangerously weaken the skeletal system. Early studies indicate that, with proper food and exercise, aging bones don't have to become porous and brittle.

Much of the research has focused on osteoporosis, a vicious age-related disease that now affects more than 20 million Americans, nine-tenths of them women. Osteoporosis usually results when bone resorption outpaces construction for a long period of time. The bones of some victims become so brittle that sitting down can break a hipbone. Especially severe in elderly women, osteoporosis is often linked with a drop in estrogen levels at menopause. Somehow the hormonal decrease appears to trigger the body to start robbing calcium from the bones. Because women generally have smaller bones than men to start with, it's no wonder that osteoporosis affects women more frequently—especially light-skinned, light-framed women who don't exercise much, and who smoke cigarettes and drink to excess. It's estimated that more than one-quarter of all women in the United States now have or will develop the disease to some extent.

Most people suffering from osteoporosis will never know it. The bone loss itself is painless, and in most cases doesn't progress far enough to cause severe problems. Many elderly people, however, will not be so lucky. Osteoporosis will contribute to some 200,000 hip fractures this year. The back is also a common target. Weakened bones in the upper spine can spontaneously collapse, leading to the hunched condition often seen in elderly women called dowager's hump.

How can this dismal future be averted? Recent findings indicate that beating age-related bone loss requires a two-pronged attack: diet and exercise. And the time to begin is when bone loss first starts, in the 30s and 40s.

DIET

Some of the most encouraging news of the past ten years concerns the role of proper diet in combating bone loss. It now appears that osteoporosis and the problems it causes are in most cases preventable.

The key is calcium. This mineral is vital for nerve conduction, muscle contraction, heartbeat, blood coagulation, immunity to disease and energy production in the body, among other things. The body uses the skeleton—two-thirds calcium salts by weight—as its calcium repository.

As we grow older, we tend to eat fewer milk products and other calcium-rich foods (see "Bone Food"). For some, the digestive system becomes increasingly intolerant of milk products as the years go by. Even when we do eat right, there's some evidence that in those more than 60 years old, the aging gut tends to absorb calcium less efficiently. Age-related hormonal changes like the menopausal drop in estrogen can worsen the problem, as can deficiencies in vitamin D, which is needed to absorb calcium. Faced with calcium deficit for whatever reason, the body begins stealing it from the bones.

BONE FOOD

According to the National Institutes of Health, American aren't getting enough calcium. Most women over 45 now consume less than 500 mg. of the mineral each day, but NIH recommends that they get at least 1,500 mg. Younger women and teenagers should get at least 1,000 mg. per day, while the current recommended daily allowance of 800 mg. is probably sufficient for most men.

To augment your calcium intake, experts recommend getting it the natural way: from your diet. The given portions of the best high-calcium foods, listed here, will each provide about 300 mg.—or about one quarter of your daily needs—of the mineral:

- One glass of whole, skim, or lowfat milk
- One cup of yogurt

- Two cups of cottage cheese
- A cup and a half of ice cream
- One and a half ounces of cheddar cheese
- One cup of cooked collard greens
- Two stalks of broccoli
- 16 medium oysters
- Four ounces of salmon canned with bones in
- Two and a half ounces of sardines

Of all these, skim milk may be the best calcium source, because it is low in calories, low in fat, and couples the mineral with vitamin D, important in helping the body absorb calcium.

Researchers are now recommending more dietary calcium than ever before, especially for pregnant and nursing women and the elderly. Studies show that increasing calcium intake in older people can slow or halt bone loss and reduce the incidence of bone fractures.

In 1980, 800 milligrams a day—the amount in about three glasses of whole milk—was considered the minimum daily requirement. But many specialists are now recommending 1,200 mg. per day for women, and up to 2,000 mg. per day for older people with evidence of bone loss. Calcium supplementation at up to 2,500 mg. per day is generally safe. But there are a few exceptions, such as people who have had trouble with calcium-containing kidney stones. Before going on a very-high-calcium regimen, talk to your doctor.

PICKING A CALCIUM SUPPLEMENT

It may be difficult for some people—especially women who need large amounts of calcium—to get all they need through diet alone. To help them, a wide variety of calcium supplements are now being sold. If you compare labels, you'll find that most use calcium in one of three basic forms:

1. **Calcium carbonate**. This group includes ground oyster shells, eggshells, and antacids like Tums. Calcium carbonate provides more calcium per unit weight than any other form, making it generally cheaper. "Natural" calcium carbonates, like those from shells and bone meal, are identical to "synthetic" forms. Some people claim that calcium carbonate antacids don't work well as calcium supplements because an acid environment is needed for calcium absorption—but researchers say this is untrue at levels required for supplementation.
2. **Calcium lactate**. Only about 13 percent of this form of supplement is actually calcium, so it takes a lot more pills to get your daily quota. As a result, it ends up costing a lot more than calcium carbonate supplements. And there's some evidence that this form and calcium gluconate may not be as effective as calcium carbonate in preventing osteoporosis.
3. **Calcium gluconate**. This form is only nine percent calcium, which means you'd have to take eight 500-mg. pills to get the same calcium in two 500-mg. calcium carbonate pills. The cost rises accordingly.

When comparing calcium supplements, check the labels to find out just how many milligrams of calcium each pill provides. And remember that both cost and effectiveness make calcium carbonate a clear winner.

One other precaution: Some stocks of "natural" sources of calcium carry the added danger of possible contamination—dolomite with uranium and oyster shells with heavy metals. Since calcium supplements made in the factory provide exactly the same benefits as those from nature, go for the safer supplements.

For women especially, adequate calcium may be difficult to get through diet alone. For those who need a calcium supplement, a wide variety of supplements have recently hit the market. Some are better than others.

EXERCISE

Research shows that bedridden patients lose bone mass much faster than those who exercise normally, and that athletes generally have denser bones than the rest of us. Some preliminary studies indicate that elderly people who begin exercising regularly can stop losing bone and even start adding it back. With the skeletal system, it looks like a case of use it or lose it.

The type of exercise is important. Even light exercise on a regular basis helps, but to do the most good, the exercises must be *weight-bearing*. Bones seem to do better when muscular stress is placed on them. The best exercises for preventing osteoporosis include:

- **Walking and light jogging**. The old standbys place maximum weight on the legs and provide some aerobic benefits as well.
- **Biking**. Even more aerobic and good for muscles in the legs.
- **Weightlifting**. Excellent for working the bones in the upper body.
- **Aerobics**. All that jumping and puffing puts stress on your bones as well as your heart.

Swimming, although great for most parts of the body, is perhaps the least effective exercise for bones: The water supports too much of your body, taking stress off the skeleton. And while the exercises listed above are good for *preventing* bone loss, people already suffering from osteoporosis should talk to a physician before beginning weightlifting or other exercises that could put too much stress on brittle bones.

THE ESTROGEN QUESTION

Diet and exercise are important in maintaining strong bones, but pinning down exactly how good they are at stopping osteoporosis will require more study. There is one therapy, however, that physicians *know* will slow the loss of bone in women: estrogen replacement.

Bone loss often worsens dramatically around the time of menopause, which in turn is caused by a decrease in estrogen, a hormone secreted by the ovaries and other tissues. Physicians for years have been replacing that lost estrogen through pills and creams as a way to lessen some of the unwanted effects of menopause (see Chapter 17).

But controversy surrounds its use for preventing osteoporosis. For one thing, no one knows *how* estrogen stops bone loss. For another, a group of researchers at the National Institute on Aging have found evidence that menopause itself doesn't cause osteoporosis. Looking at data from more than 7,000 cases, they discovered that the rate of hip fractures for white women, typically used as an indicator of osteoporosis, starts a steep rise just after age 40—nearly a decade earlier than the average age of menopause. There was no sharp increase in the rate at the age of menopause. The researchers concluded that more attention should be paid to preventing osteoporosis through altered diet and exercise habits earlier in life.

And estrogen therapy has its risks. Although different than those associated with estrogen-containing birth-control pills, the dangers of postmenopausal estrogen-replacement therapy can still be significant for some women. They include increased risks of high blood pressure, endometrial cancer and gallstone formation.

A recent consensus conference at the National Institutes of Health concluded that estrogen therapy to prevent osteoporosis was "highly effective" and warranted for women whose ovaries had been removed before age 50. For women going through natural menopause, the recommendation was a bit more cautious, okaying estrogen replacement as long as the patients understood the risks and were examined regularly. The panel added, however, that "Until more data on risks and benefits are available, physicians and patients may prefer to reserve estrogen...for conditions that confer a high risk of osteoporosis, such as the occurrence of premature menopause." Other experts echo that note of caution, stressing that estrogen-replacement therapy should be considered only in carefully selected cases.

THE SPINE

Of all the bones in the body, none are more important for long-term health and good looks than those in the spinal column. And nothing better illustrates the interplay between bone and other parts of the body—muscle, nerve and ligament—in maintaining youthful health.

This exquisitely engineered, delicately curved stack of 33 bones (each one called a vertebra) supports us, protects vital nerves in the spinal cord, serves as an attachment point for important muscles and cushions the bumps of life. The S-shape of the spine, bending back at the shoulders and forward in the small of the back, helps it absorb the shock of walking upright. Spongy discs of tissue between each of the vertebra (called intervertebral discs) help cushion the back as well.

Unfortunately, the pressures we put on this engineering marvel make it easy to throw our backs out of whack. Few among us haven't either suffered from painful back problems or known someone who has.

Many of these problems are tied to simple mechanical stress. The backbone carries almost all of the weight of the upper body concentrated in a relatively small area. Think of the spine as a mast carrying all the sails, spars and rigging—the muscle, bones and organs—that make up the upper body. In that soft area between the rib cage and pelvis, the backbone alone carries the weight. That's enough stress as it is, but add to it the tremendous pull of the many muscles and liagaments that strain against the back to keep us upright.

Think of the mast again. It can't stand by itself. It has to be held upright by two opposing forces: the forward pull of a line between the mast and the bow of the ship, and the backward pull of the stern line. If either line is too tight or too loose, the mast sways out of position.

It's the same with the back. Most of our body weight, as well as our strong abdominal muscles, are in front of the spine, pulling us forward. This is balanced by an intricate system of extremely strong muscles and ligaments behind the spine that pull us back.

Unfortunately, it's all too easy to throw off this balancing act. When that happens, nerves running down and branching from the spine can signal pain. At some point, eight of ten Americans will be wracked by a back problem—tens of millions badly enough to be incapacitated. Back problems are the number-one cause of lost work time in the United States.

And aging doesn't help. Age-related degeneration of the bones, muscles and ligaments of the back can lead to a painful, stooped posture and loss of height. Happily, we can take preventive measures now.

BACK PROBLEMS

The shrinking of stature and the bent frame so often associated with old age result from three basic processes: disc degeneration and flattening; crushed vertebrae due to osteoporosis; and a general loosening of ligaments and muscles that hold the back in place.

Disc Degeneration

The spongy intervertebral discs that separate and cushion the bones of the back tend to gradually flatten out. We can see the effects of disc-flattening every morning. After a night's rest from the battle with gravity, discs expand, and we're actually one-half to three-quarters of an inch taller in the morning than the night before. Astronauts in space can "grow" up to two inches in height while freed from gravity's pull.

Of course, we can't spend our lives in outer space. Here on earth, daily life as an upright being takes its toll by gradually pushing down the intervertebral discs. Each disc consists of a soft, jellylike center surrounded by a tough ring of fiber. The center absorbs the shocks, the fibrous ring keeps the center from squishing out of place.

But occasionally there's a blowout: The center will rupture the fibrous ring and form a blisterlike bulge. This is a *herniated disc*—also called, improperly, a *slipped disc*—a condition that can be extremely painful if the bulging disc hits a nearby nerve.

Oddly, herniated discs are one back condition we can worry about less as we age. When we're young, discs are 90% water. But in our 20s, they start a decades-long process of drying out and shrinking, a process that makes them tougher and less likely to rupture. Herniated discs most commonly affect people in their 20s, 30s and 40s, especially those who sit all day at a desk or drive motor vehicles for a living. After age 60, a ruptured disc is a rarity. But disc shrinkage is also one reason we grow shorter late in life. And there's not much we can do about it.

Age-related changes in discs are linked to two other problems that often get worse with age:

- *Degenerative arthritis.* If we live long enough, there's a good chance we'll suffer from it to some extent. Also known as osteoarthritis, degenerative joint disease, and perhaps most accurately as wear-and-tear arthritis, this condition seems to be the simple result of using our joints. This condition, discussed in more detail in Chapter 11, can lead to general creakiness and stiffness in old age.
- *Rheumatoid arthritis.* This is a much more serious disease, although it affects fewer people (about 6.5 million in the U.S., three-quarters of them women). This disease, also discussed in more detail in Chapter 12, usually spreads to the back only after it affects other joints. But when it does, it can be a crippler. Rheumatoid arthritis can eat away intervertebral discs, damage bone, and allow vertebrae to settle painfully on one another. Unfortunately, because the causes of rheumatoid arthritis are unknown, prevention is difficult.

Crushed Vertebrae

The ravages of osteoporosis can result in a spontaneous fracturing of weakened vertebrae. Bones in the neck can become so porous that they collapse under the weight they carry. These compression fractures can crush the neck bones into wedge shapes, leading to a painfully hunched upper-back condition commonly called dowager's hump. And crushed vertebrae are more than painful: When one or two go, they can shrink a person's height by several inches over time. That shrinkage can compress the space the lungs have to work in, increasing the chances of some lung diseases.

Weak Muscles and Ligaments

The third cause of stooping and loss of height is the age-related weakening of the intricate system of muscles and ligaments that holds our spines in place. Responsible for keeping us upright by balancing the forward pull of our weight and posture, these muscles and ligaments are subject to tremendous strain. Over time, unless they're taken care of, these support tissues can grow lax, allowing our back and neck to bend out of position, speeding the processes of degenerative arthritis and disc problems. See more on this in Chapter 13.

THE SOLUTIONS

Now is the time to start a regimen of diet and exercise designed to prevent many of the ills that old-age backs are heir to. Although back problems are highly individual, a few general tips can serve to keep all backs in better shape.

EXERCISE

Experts agree that a sensible program of regular physical activity will help keep the back in proper shape. Exercise helps keep weight down, and back problems are more common among people who are overweight. Remember the analogy of the ship's mast: The more weight the spine has to support in front, the more the back muscles and ligaments have to compensate by tightening behind the spine—thus greatly increasing the total pressure on your back. The worst offender is that bane of the American male, the potbelly. An extra ten pounds carried ten inches in front of your spine translates into an extra *fifty* pounds of pressure on your lower back.

Keeping in good general shape can also prevent the "tired back" syndrome that so many physicians see—people with nagging backaches that disappear as soon as they start regular exercise. The most important set of muscles to keep in shape are not the back muscles—these get exercise every time we move—but the stomach muscles. Weak stomach muscles allow the stomach to stick out and the lower back to sag—throwing the entire back out of balance. The best exercises for toning your stomach are presented in "Stomach Strengtheners for Your Back," below.

STOMACH STRENGTHENERS FOR YOUR BACK

The most important exercises for a healthy back, according to the American Medical Association, are those that strengthen the stomach muscles. To keep your abdominals in shape, physicians recommend some simple variations on the common sit-up. Work your way comfortably down this list of exercises of increasing difficulty. Start slowly with a few repetitions at one level. When you can do 20 successively, move to the next exercise:

- Lying flat on your back, tilt your pelvis so the small of the back is as close as possible to the ground, then raise your head far enough to look at your feet.
- Again on your back, arms at your sides, knees bent, raise your head and shoulders about six inches off the ground, hands reaching toward the calves. Hold for one to three seconds. Hooking your feet under the bed or a bar is cheating—it lets your thigh muscles do the work instead of your stomach muscles.
- The full sit-up starts the same way, but continues until your head reaches your knees.

Other variations on the sit-up include clasping the hands behind the head or on the chest. Remember: Include stomach exercises in a regular exercise routine, make the stomach muscles do the work—and stop if there's pain.

Pelvic tilts are another important group of exercises for preventing lower-back pain and keeping the spine in alignment. Because strong back muscles pull the spine backward, the lower back has a tendency to curve inward more than it should. Pelvic tilts are designed to counter that tendency by loosening and limbering the lower back muscles.

For those with some lower-back pain already, physicians recommend simply lying on the back, arms at the side, and raising both knees to the chest. Pull them in as tight as possible with your arms. You'll feel the lower back stretching and flattening to the floor. A more strenuous version for those with healthy backs is the old standby of calisthenics, the standing toe-touch. Stand straight, arms at your side. Now bend at the waist, reaching fingers to toes.

Observe these precautions while exercising for a healthy back:

- **Develop your own exercise routine.** It's a good idea to exercise at least three times a week, but everyone has a different back with different exercise capabilities. When starting a regular program of exercise, begin slowly and work up gradually. The most common cause of back pain is simply overworked muscles due to improper or overdone exercises.
- **If it hurts, don't do it.** Exercise up to the level where strain is evident—not over that level. Joggers often ignore this advice, running despite nagging lower-back pain. It only gets worse, often resulting in incapacitation for weeks. According to *Runner's World* magazine, "runner's back" will soon rival runner's knee as a top problem for long-distance athletes. "No pain, no gain" is advice for masochists, not you. When your back sends a pain message, ease up.
- **Strengthen your stomach and limber your back.** The idea is to equalize the forward and backward pulls on your spine. Besides the exercises already listed, yoga, stretching, swimming, gymnastics and dance all help strengthen and limber muscles equilaterally.
- **Lift with care.** The farther away a lifted object is from your body, the more stress it puts on your back. Squat by the object, keep it close to your body and lift with your legs, not your back.

POSTURE

Forget everything your parents and teachers taught you about good posture. Sitting up straight is bad. Shoulders back, chest out is bad. Elbows off the table is bad. The old rules about good posture were designed more for military discipline than good health. Now physicians and therapists have found that the best posture relieves pressure on the back and prevents spinal sagging, especially the lower-back condition called swayback.

To test your posture, stand normally, back against a wall. Your upper back and buttocks should touch the wall. Now slip your hand in the space between your lower back and the wall. It should fit easily, almost touching on both sides. If there's a lot of extra room, you're arching your lower back excessively.

To get a feeling for how to correct this, move your feet out from the wall an inch or two without bending your hips or knees and with your buttocks and upper back still in place. You'll have to tuck your tailbone under, flattening your lower back to the wall. This pelvic tilt relieves pressure on the lower back, limbers the muscles—and helps prevent back problems.

Good posture means standing easily and gracefully, pelvis forward. Don't accentuate any abnormal curve to the spine by hunching forward or letting the stomach protrude. When standing for a long period of time—whether ironing, washing dishes, or working at a workbench—take a tip from your local tavern: Raise one leg slightly, as on the footrail of a bar. This helps relieve pressure on the lower back, and can be done easily with a low stool or box.

Good posture while sitting is even more important. Although it seems like common sense that sitting would ease pressure on the back, the opposite is true. Sitting shifts the center of gravity forward, and back muscles have to pull back to keep you upright. One study has shown that sitting with your back unsupported places 40% more stress on your lower back than standing. This helps explain why office workers have higher rates of back problems than workers in many more strenuous trades.

For the desk-bound, fitness experts offer these solutions:

- **Move around**. Whether in an office or in a car, try not to sit for more than an hour at a time. Get up and stretch or take a short walk. Shift in your seat. Lean forward and put your elbows on the table. Lean back and—if the boss isn't watching—put your feet up. A good exercise while sitting is to bend forward, getting your head as close as possible to the knees, arms dangling. This stretches out the lower back and relieves pressure.

- **Choose a good chair**. The rule is go for comfort. Each person has a favorite chair, like John Kennedy's wooden rocker. Find yours. Look for the following:
    * Good back support, especially for the lower back.
    * A height that lets your feet rest firmly on the floor without dangling.
    * Armrests that help take some of he weight off your back.
    * A seat size, front to back, that supports your thighs fully without forcing your legs out.
- **Care for your back even while sleeping**. Good posture applies both night and day. The worst way to sleep, back experts say, is on your stomach. This tends to exaggerate the curve in the lower back and the problems that can cause. An ideal sleeping posture is on your side, in an almost fetal position with hips and knees bent forward. This can be done on your back, too, if you put pillows or some other support under your knees. This position tends to flatten and relieve pressure on the lower back. But again, whatever's comfortable goes. As long as you awaken with no back problems, why change? Unfortunately, a bad bed can aggravate a bad back regardless of posture. Generally, firmer beds tend to be better for backs because they don't allow you to sag into unnatural positions. But if you put a board under your mattress and wake up the next morning in pain—go back to whatever keeps you the happiest.

11

Joints

Any good mechanic will tell you moving parts wear out first. And many older people, thinking of their aching, creaking joints, would agree. Joints are the moving parts of the human body. They work like machinery and are named like machinery: ball-and-socket joints (hips and shoulder), hinge joints (elbow and knee), gliding, pivot and saddle joints.

But unlike the moving parts of machines, joints *don't* wear out first. With a little care and activity, your joints will last you painlessly your entire life.

That's not to say they won't change. With age, the tissues surrounding the joints begin to fray and erode, and bones can alter their shape. On X-rays, 90 percent of all people show at least a small degree of joint degeneration by age 40. Joint changes on an X-ray, however, do not mean that you'll suffer any pain or discomfort at all. A little joint deterioration is a normal part of aging.

Unfortunately, for millions of Americans, joint-related problems can make later life a torture. Various forms of arthritis can, if we're not careful (and, in susceptible people, even if we are) lead to sore, creaking joints and stooped stature. Some types of arthritis are preventable, some aren't. But the feeling that nothing can be done about joint diseases—that a gradual loss of flexibility and increasing joint discomfort is a natural part of aging—is just plain wrong. By exercising, watching closely for problems and treating joints carefully, most people can be assured of a lifetime of comfortable and easy movement.

WHY GOOD JOINTS GO BAD

Scientists classify any place in the body where two bones meet as a joint. But just because it's called a joint doesn't mean it moves. The meeting places where pieces of our skull are sutured together are immovable joints. Other joints move very little, like those holding the two bones in our lower arms in place.

But the joints that matter most in aging are those that determine how easily and fluidly we move—highly flexible joints like those in the finger, knee, elbow, hip and shoulder. At these points in the body, bones have to be held firmly together, yet allowed to move freely—to be in tight proximity, yet not rub against each other. The body solves these problems by wrapping the joints in a bag or capsule of strong ligament and collagen that holds the bones near one another, yet allows a small space for movement between them. Tear that bag by wrenching the joint out of place, and you have a dislocated shoulder or knee.

Bones shouldn't rub against each other. When they do, they wear away or begin adding bone to form odd-shaped spurs. To prevent rubbing, the ends of the bones in movable joints are lined with a layer of cartilage that pads and cushions them, allowing them to slide more easily. The joint is also oiled with a slippery lubricant much like egg white, which is secreted from the surrounding capsule.

It all works fine—for about the first 20 years of life. After that, the ligaments and cartilage in the joints begin to show signs of aging. They discolor and begin to fray. In our 30s and 40s, nearly all of us, whether we know it or not, begin to suffer from one form or another of joint change.

Most of these long-term joint problems are collectively called arthritis, an umbrella term for more than 100 different diseases. Arthritis, which literally means the inflammation of a joint, can have effects that range from trivial to crippling, depending on the specific type of disease involved. Chances are if we live long enough, we'll eventually suffer from some form of arthritis.

Unfortunately, the causes of many forms of arthritis are still unknown, and there's no proven cure for any of them. That means the best way to keep joints healthy is through prevention, by exercising carefully and staying alert for signs of the onset of arthritic conditions. Once a joint is arthritic, it can't be made healthy again—but it can be treated so that it won't get worse.

Two forms of arthritis account for the lion's share of problems in the United States. Degenerative joint disease (DJD) is most closely tied to normal aging. Rheumatoid arthritis is far more severe and seems to be tied to the immune system.

DEGENERATIVE JOINT DISEASE

This is a disease of many names: osteoarthritis, degenerative arthritis, wear-and-tear arthritis. Technically, it shouldn't be called arthritis at all, because it usually doesn't involve the inflammation of a joint.

DJD is often fingered as the main reason most old folks are stiff when they get out of bed in the morning, have chronically aching backs or cricks in their necks. But it usually is not—in most cases, the aches and pains of growing old have less to do with joint deterioration and more to do with muscles, ligaments and tendons stiffened from years of underuse.

Still, DJD is the most common type of structural joint problem in the United States, hitting 16 million Americans—mostly elderly—hard enough to be somewhat debilitating. Despite the numbers, it's also the least serious type of joint disease.

Degenerative joint disease seems to be caused by simply using the joints. Every time we move, the cartilage pads on the ends of the bones have a chance to rub together. Eventually they start to wear out, and the underlying bone begins to change shape. In some cases, potentially painful bone spurs begin to grow.

Some older studies supported what logic would dictate: The problem is most common among people who use their joints most, such as laborers involved in physically demanding jobs, and worst in the joints receiving the most wear and tear—knees, fingers, the lower back and the area just below the neck. A famous study charted the increased incidence of back problems among coal miners in Britain. The lesson seemed to be: Use it *and* lose it.

But more recent studies have indicated just the opposite. For one thing, there seems to be a hereditary factor involved, since two people doing the same kind of work for the same period of time often don't suffer the same degree of degeneration. For another, studies on athletes indicate that careful joint use can actually decrease problems rather than make them worse. Weightlifters in one study had fewer back problems than nonlifters. Long-term joggers have been found to have no more DJD in their legs than inactive people. The key seems to be what the type of activity is and how it is performed.

To make sure you don't suffer unnecessarily from DJD, try the following:

- **Exercise carefully.** A complete exercise program should include a way of stretching and limbering your joints. The section on "Exercise and your joints" at the end of this chapter gives more suggestions on dos and don'ts.
- **Vary your work routine.** Many jobs put repetitive strain on one or a few joints—and those that are used most are most likely to degenerate. Coal miners who use their backs a lot have been found to have a higher rate of degenerative joint disease in their lower backs. Give your most used joints a break: If you're stuck at a keyboard all day, stop often to stretch your finger joints; if you're tied to a desk, try to make sure you get up and take some pressure off your lower spine.
- **Watch your weight.** Excess weight adds stress to all weight-bearing joints.
- **Watch your posture.** Poor standing or sitting postures can put extra strain on joints in the back and hips. Some tips for good posture can be found in Chapter 11.

RHEUMATOID ARTHRITIS

Although it affects far fewer people than degenerative joint disease (about 6.5 million people versus some 40 million), rheumatoid arthritis is a far more serious problem. It hits victims mainly between the ages of 20 and 50, and it hits hard: Affected joints are eaten away and destroyed. Victims are crippled and may suffer bodywide fatigue, fever and weight loss.

No one knows what causes it. The most popular theory is that it is an autoimmune disease—one in which the body's defense system turns against something in the joints, eventually destroying them. New research has found that genetics may be important as well. The disease is often associated with a particular protein on cell surfaces common among rheumatoid arthritis victims but rare among those who don't get the disease. For reasons not yet understood, women are affected three times more often than men. Fingers, wrists, elbows, hips, knees and ankles are the joints most commonly afflicted.

Although there is no cure, rheumatoid arthritis can be kept under control through early detection and quick treatment. Early diagnosis is especially important because damage to a joint can often be stopped, but it can't be reversed. Unfortunately, people with symptoms of arthritis wait an average of four years before they seek help—and that may be four years too late.

The National Institute on Aging recommends checking with a physician if any of the following early warning signs of arthritis persist for more than six weeks:

- Pain, tenderness or swelling in one or more joints.
- Pain and stiffness in the morning.
- Recurring or persistent pain and stiffness in the neck, lower back or knees.
- Symptoms such as these that go away for a week or month but return.

When rheumatoid arthritis is discovered, it can be treated by using drugs to fight the destructive inflammation—aspirin is the most common—and special combinations of exercise and rest to prevent pain and keep the joint from deteriorating further. In severe cases, physicians use stronger treatments directed against the immune system, including gold therapy and anticancer drugs.

Research is now targeted toward getting at the roots of this disease. Scientists are looking at the immune system, the role of genetics and the possibility that rheumatoid arthritis may be triggered by an infectious agent like a virus. Although diet doesn't seem to play an important role in preventing the disease, one group of medical scientists has found that eating special oils called omega-threes, found in fish and other seafoods, may help relieve the pain and inflammation associated with the disease. More information on omega-threes can be found in Chapter 15.

Perhaps the biggest danger surrounding rheumatoid arthritis is rampant quackery. Sufferers spend millions of dollars every year on everything from electro-belts to nutritional cures. None of it works, and it prevents arthritis patients from seeking medical help that can potentially stop the disease's progress.

EXERCISE AND YOUR JOINTS

The American way of exercise emphasizes looks and sweat—and generally ignores the needs of our joints. Pumping iron to build masses of muscle, jogging to stay lean, playing tennis to look good at the club are all fine in moderation, but if improperly done can lead to joint problems.

SPORTS TO WATCH OUT FOR

Any repetitive, chronic stress on a particular joint can wear it out if proper precautions aren't taken. To keep your joints healthier longer, play the following sports carefully and in moderation:

- *Football* adds injury to insult. In addition to putting repeated intense stress on knee, ankle and shoulder joints, the sport requires crashing into things and falling down. Football players have joint problems not because they wear out—they don't last long enough for that—but because they're dislocated, sprained, smashed and broken.
- *Basketball* players know what goes first: the knees. Constant jumping stresses ankles, too, resulting in a plethora of sprains, bone spurs and breaks. The problem again is damage rather than long-term wear.
- *Tennis* has a degenerative joint condition named after it. But tennis elbow results from improper use of the joint rather than overuse, and most often affects people who play infrequently or incorrectly. To avoid it, take lessons from a pro to learn proper technique, play regularly to hone skills and keep your arm muscles in shape, and buy a racket fitted to your grip.
- *Jogging* can come with its own list of chronic leg and foot problems if it's improperly done. But a long-term study has shown that joggers suffer no more joint problems than their sedentary peers if they take a few precautions: Shoes must be top-quality and well-fitted, and beginners

must work up slowly to longer distances. The key is getting in shape gradually rather than pushing yourself too fast. For information on shinsplints, see Chapter 12.

- *Raquetball* players can put intense stress on their knees and ankles because of the quick stops and turns required by the game. Again, learn from an expert, wear proper shoes and get in shape slowly.

Instead of ignoring joints, exercise programs should include components designed to keep them limber and healthy. Lack of flexibility is one tell-tale sign of old age—and one that proper exercise can help us avoid. Take the following tips into account when devising an exercise routine:

- Don't stop yourself from doing *any* pleasurable physical activity—but get into each form of exercise gradually. Your brain may tell you that you can jog as if you're 20 years old when you start at age 35—but your body knows better.
- Stretching should be an integral part of any exercise program. Joints respond best to gentle stretching done after a short warm-up period that gets the blood circulating. The idea is to keep the joints moving freely and completely by carefully elongating the tendons, muscles and ligaments that surround the joint. Always stretch slowly and hold the extended position; never bounce or jerk the joint. The older you are, the longer you should spend warming up and stretching (see Chapter 12).
- Try to stretch all major joints equally rather than putting constant stress on just a few—as joggers do on knees and hips, or weightlifters on elbows and shoulders. Hatha yoga is an ideal limbering and stretching regimen for the joints.
- Don't overexercise. Research has shown that too much exercise squeezes the lubricant out of the joints. The less lubricant there is, the easier it is to abrade the cartilage padding. When your body says stop, stop. You're not a professional athlete paid to "play through" pain.
- Don't underexercise. The quickest way to cause severe joint deterioration is to stop using the joint entirely—as anyone who's been bedridden can attest. The reason may be tied to that same lubricating fluid, which researchers have found to build up in joints

when they're underused. The build-up seems to be the first sign of underused joint problems. And underuse leads to stiff, tight muscles, ligaments and tendons that can eventually give you that creaky, achey feeling so many people blame on "old age."

A QUICK WHOLE-BODY STRETCH

There are as many stretching regimens as there are exercise teachers, but the following list will provide a basic stretch for the major joints of your body. Remember to stretch slowly and fluidly, hold the extended position for several seconds and *never* hold a position that is painful. Researchers now recommend doing your stretches after a brief warm-up to get the blood moving.

1. **Neck**. Standing straight, carefully roll your head and neck, looking down at your feet first, then bringing your right ear as close to your right shoulder as possible, stretching your head back, then left ear to left shoulder. Repeat in the opposite direction.
2. **Shoulders and arms**. Still standing, reach toward the ceiling with the right arm, stretching as far as you can. Lower it, repeat with the left. To go a step further, join your hands above your head, arms straight, and bend to either side until you feel your side muscles stretch.
3. **Back and thighs**. Standing with feet together, bend at the waist and reach for your toes. This stretches both the back and the back of the legs. A variation on this can be done sitting on the floor, legs straight in front of you. Again, bend at the waist, reach for the toes and grasp your legs as far down as you can reach. Pull your body down toward the legs and hold. To stretch the back the other way, stand, clasp your hands above the head, arms straight, and arch backward.
4. **Calves**. After stretching the back of the legs as described above, do a traditional jogger's stretch by leaning against a wall at a 45-degree angle, hands on the

wall, one leg bent, the other stretched straight with the foot flat on the floor. Reverse legs and repeat.

5. **Hips**. Sitting in a chair, place your right ankle on your left knee, and gently push down on your right knee until you feel the stretch. Hold. Repeat, reversing the legs.

12
Muscle

It is burned into the minds of most American males: A skinny weakling in a swimsuit wipes sand and tears out of his eyes as his girl friend recedes down the beach, arm-in-arm with a muscle-bound chunk of prime beefcake. Humiliation. But wait—a few weeks later, thanks to the right comic-book body building course, the weakling is a rebuilt, self-assured he-man. One look at his brawny biceps, and back comes the girl.

The moral? Muscle is what you need. Nurtured on that idea, millions of American men—and, increasingly, women—have taken to the weight room to create the body beautiful.

Weight-bearing exercise, including weight lifting, does help keep muscle and bone healthy. The more lean muscle you have instead of fat, the more calories your body will burn, and the easier it is to stay slim.

But pumping enough iron to look like Arnold Schwarzenegger isn't essential, either for winning affection or maintaining good health. In fact, muscle is one of the easiest tissues of the body to keep in shape as we age. With some understanding of how it works and a bit of regular care, your muscular system will keep you moving well and looking good until late in life.

WHAT MUSCLES ARE

Nearly half of an adult's body weight consists of muscle, including *heart* muscle, discussed in Chapter 15, and *visceral* muscles, found in the walls of blood vessels, the stomach and intestines. But when we think of muscles, we usually think of the largest and most visible group: skeletal muscles. These are the stomach muscles we struggle to flatten, the biceps we strain to build, the thigh muscles we sweat to tone. They also include muscles we don't think much about: the tiny muscles that control eye movements, the diaphragm muscle that helps us breathe.

All muscles have three things in common: They can shorten, usually when triggered by a nerve impulse; they can stretch; and they're elastic enough to return to their normal shape after either movement.

Muscle cells can do all this thanks to filaments within each cell that slide over each other, drawing together when a nerve impulse tells the muscle to tighten, and sliding apart for a stretch. Each nerve controls a packet of muscle cells ranging from 10 cells per nerve in the eye to 500 per nerve in the leg. When the nerve says go, the whole packet tightens as much as it can for as long as it can before relaxing. With muscle cell contractions, it's an all-or-nothing situation.

A continuous effort, like gripping this book, is possible when nerves fire one after another, tightening one small packet of muscle cells as another tires. A greater effort contracts more packets more often. This sequence of tightening and relaxing goes on at a low level all the time, even during sleep. The result is what we call muscle tone.

Because muscle cells, like brain cells, can't make more of themselves, the number you have shortly after birth is the number you'll have to work with all your life. So how can the weakling on the beach turn into a hunk? Exercise can't change the *number* of muscle cells you've got, but it can change the *size* of each cell. Well-exercised muscle cells contain more contractile protein and enzymes to help them work better. Bigger cells bunch up more when they contract, giving a more impressive flex. Exercise can also increase the blood flow to muscles, "pumping" them up in size.

Blood brings food and oxygen to the muscle cells. The food can come from a variety of sources—blood sugar, carbohydrates, protein, fat—depending on how hard and how long the muscles work. But oxygen is vital at every step. When you start exercising strenuously, it takes time for your body to gear up to what you're asking your muscles to do. It may take several minutes after you've started jogging, for instance, for your heartbeat and breathing to increase enough to provide all the oxygen needed by your muscles.

During the low-oxygen period, your muscles work without breathing. It's called *anaerobic* exercise, and it produces a chemical by-product called lactic acid that can build up in muscles and prevent them from working efficiently. Lactic acid build-up is a major reason muscles get tired.

But sufficient oxygen breaks down lactic acid. Once your heart starts pumping faster and your breathing speeds up, more oxygen is rushed to working muscle. Now your muscles can produce energy without building up lactic acid. You're doing what's called *aerobic* exercise.

And that's why a healthy heart and lungs are so important in making muscles work well. If your cardiovascular system isn't in shape to do its oxygen-supplying job efficiently, you end up panting and tiring easily.

NORMAL AGING

Muscle cells are hardy. Studies show that, in the absence of disease or injury, most people don't lose an appreciable number of muscle cells with normal aging.

But that doesn't mean you won't get weaker or your muscles won't get smaller. Both happen as each of those long-lived muscle cells shrinks. Studies show that the handgrip strength of people in their 80s is only about half that of people in their 30s. Most of this weakening happens after age 60; until then, most people maintain about 90 percent of their maximum strength. Loss of power goes hand-in-hand with a gradual loss of overall muscle mass. Both men and women lose muscle at about the same rate.

Along with the decline of strength is an increase of water, fat and other non-muscle tissue in the muscles of older people. One study found that fat constituted one-third of the calf muscle in a group of people between 70 and 80 years of age. Within the muscle cells, there also appears to be a decrease in the important enzymes used to turn food and oxygen into energy. Some scientists think that the slowing and gradual loss of muscle-related nerves may be important. Others look to age-related hormonal changes as the key.

But a basic problem lies in distinguishing how much of this decline is due to aging itself from how much is due to a lack of exercise. Some physiologists now say that 50 percent of a person's functional decline is due to inactivity. Underscoring that observation is the fact that unexercised muscles quickly begin to atrophy. They lose protein, shrink in size and diminish in strength. It's clearly a case of use it or lose it. And studies show that older people just don't use their muscles enough.

THE IMPORTANCE OF EXERTION

There are many excuses for not exercising as we age, ranging from stiff joints and shortness of breath to a frighteningly thumping heart. Besides, old people look ridiculous when they exercise, and old age is a time to slow down right?

Not if you want to age well. As Chapters 11 and 14 show, normal age-related changes in joints, the heart and lung aren't an excuse. For most people, the real problem with exercising is a lifetime of *not* exercising.

Underexercised hearts and lungs don't bring enough oxygen to muscle cells. Less oxygen to the muscles means less get-up-and-go and a decrease in stamina, the ability to do sustained muscular work. Without stamina, exercise becomes a pain rather than a pleasure.

So older people exercise less. With less exercise, muscle decreases in size and fat increases. Because muscle burns more calories pound-for-pound than fat, the gradual loss of muscle means that the body's metabolism slows down. At age 30, it takes more than 1,600 calories per day on an average just to maintain the body, without exercise. By age 80 this drops to barely more than 1,300 calories per day. The fewer calories you burn, the more likely it is you'll put on weight—and the heavier you are, the more difficult it is to exercise.

It's a vicious circle, but you can break it.

New evidence shows that your body's ability to use oxygen depends on the amount you exercise, not the other way around. Look at aerobic capacity, the amount of oxygen your body burns per minute during peak exertion, adjusted for your size. A higher aerobic capacity generally reflects large lung capacity, a strong heart, a good blood supply and healthy muscles and enzymes. And researchers have found that an active 60-year-old can have a higher aerobic capacity than a couch-potato 20-year-old.

Another bit of evidence supporting the importance of exercise comes from looking at muscles that are well-exercised regardless of health habits. Heart and diaphragm muscles work 24 hours a day—and appear to age more slowly than underused skeletal muscles.

The body retains its ability to respond to exercise until very late in life. This is especially true of the heart-lung system that is the basis of aerobic capacity. Researchers have found that beginning a proper exercise regimen can boost your aerobic capacity at almost any age and quickly begin undoing long-term neglect. A well-maintained program can keep aerobic capacity high. The ability to shrink fat cells through exercise and build up the enzymes important in helping to change oxygen into energy is also maintained until very old age. Regular endurance exercise—jogging, swimming, walking, and so on—can double the oxygen-burning capacity of muscle. And that means muscles that fatigue less easily.

While the case for revitalizing aerobic capacity is clear, the data on building muscle itself is mixed. Some reports indicate that you can beef up muscle cells with exercise at almost any age. But other researchers disagree. One study found that an age-related build-up of fat happened in much-used muscles—such as those in the larynx and eye—at the same rate as underused muscles. Another found that, despite exercise, a group of physically active older men had no more muscle mass than did their nonactive peers—although they *did* have less fat and a leaner look. And, at least in very old age, it appears that some loss of muscle mass and strength is probably inevitable.

While it may not be possible to build a Mister Universe body at 50, researchers agree that regular exercise is vital for keeping muscles in good shape. The question is, what kind of exercise, and when?

THE RIGHT STUFF FOR MUSCLES

You think you've got it made. You were a top athlete in college, working out every day, building a muscular body, keeping slim. It should be easy to keep in shape the rest of your life.

Not so. At middle age, according to one study, the typical university athlete is less active, heavier and more likely to smoke and drink than his or her nonsporting classmates. That's not to say that early exercise isn't important. Physiologists believe that building the body's musculature and aerobic capacity early in life can help offset later declines. But the key is maintaining a regular exercise regimen throughout your life, coupled with the right diet and moderate personal habits.

Unfortunately, most of us don't keep up our exercise. One in four people in their early 20s spend more than three hours per week in some form of vigorous exercise; less than one in 15 in their late 60s do the same.

Exercise physiologists believe the best exercises are those you enjoy doing, that can be done in moderation throughout life and that benefit the heart and lungs as well as muscles.

Weight lifting doesn't fit the bill because it gives little push to the heart and lungs. That's not to say that weight lifting is something to avoid. It builds strength, tones and shapes muscles and, in moderation, can be an important part of an overall exercise program.

PUMPING IRON

Weight lifting isn't the ideal exercise for overall muscle fitness, but it does build strength and gives devotees an alternative to singles bars. If you're new to the sport, experts recommend the following schedule to get in shape:

1. The first two months, build your muscle bulk. Work with a trainer who can show you how to use the equipment properly, then use weights that allow you to do 12-20 repetitions of a lift without groaning and giving up.

2. The next two months, work on endurance. Drop the weight to a point where you can do 40-50 repetitions without stopping.

3. Finally, build strength. Go to heavier weights that challenge you to do 2-6 repetitions. As you develop your muscles, constantly increase the size of the weights.

But strength is only one component of what you want muscles to do. The other things you should think about are:

- *Power*—defined as the amount of strength exerted over a period of time. The faster you are at a given strength level, the more power you can exert. Weight training won't make you quick or give you agility.
- *Skill*—something that comes from thinking about and practicing a difficult physical task, such as playing tennis or skiing. Weight lifting is all brawn, little brains.
- *Stamina*—a measure of how long you can last, is tied to aerobic capacity, and weight lifting comes up short in the aerobic department.

To work on all these, pick a combination of exercises that will hold your interest and provide as much of each benefit as possible. Close-to-perfect exercises include cross-country skiing, jogging, swimming and biking.

How much how often? Maintaining good health doesn't require much. Exercise experts recommend the equivalent of about a *half-hour* of brisk walking *every other day* for aerobic benefits, coupled with stretching and flexibility exercises on off days (see Chapter 11). The "equivalent" can be anything that causes deep breathing and sweating, without causing great discomfort. Or you can calculate what's aerobic and what's not by charting your heart rate (see Chapter 6).

But getting into good shape will take something more. Working up to a *half-hour* of strenuous aerobic exercise *every day*, preceded by a warmup and stretch, and followed by a cool-down and stretch, is a good starting place. The stress is on the phrase "working up." Jumping full-tilt into a new aerobic activity can do more harm than good. Beginning joggers, for instance, should start with no more than ten minutes per session, and add no more than 20 percent to that time in any week.

Warm-ups, cool-downs and stretches are vital. A 10-minute walk or slow bike ride to wherever you're exercising, or a few minutes of light jogging in place will serve for a warm-up. The idea is to get your blood pumping, start your heartbeat and breathing toward the rates you're going to ask of them and switch your muscles from an anaerobic to an aerobic mode.

Stretching muscles after a warm-up will help prevent muscle tears and joint injury. Researchers recommend no less than 15 minutes of stretching before exercise for people older than 35. Well-stretched muscles will suffer from pulls and strains less.

When you've finished the strenuous portion of your aerobic routine, take a five-minute walk to cool down and allow your cardiovascular system slowly to come back to normal. End with another stretch—researchers are now stressing the importance of stretching *after* exercising to prevent cramps and keep muscles in good shape for next time.

CRAMPS, PULLS AND SHINSPLINTS

Exercise is good, but exercising the wrong way can damage muscles. And muscles aren't shy about telling you when they're hurting: You'll feel the sharp clutch of a cramp, the ache of a pull, the stabbing of shinsplints either right away or the next night or day.

- *Cramps* happen when an unnatural position or a lack of blood flow after exercise causes muscles to tighten uncontrollably. The best antidote is immediately stretching the cramped muscle—it seems to break the cycle of misfiring nerves that tell the muscle to tighten. Night cramps afflict many people, especially pregnant women and the elderly, hitting the calf or foot most often; these are usually linked to blankets that push the foot into a bad position. Extra vitamins can help (see below), as can using a small piece of board to prop up the blankets at the foot of the bed.
- *Pulled muscles* are the result of improper or inadequate stretching. When you ask an unstretched, cold muscle to do work suddenly, you risk putting so much stress on it that the fibers are damaged. In severe muscle pulls, the muscle can tear. It's one of the worst things you can do to a muscle. The scar tissue that forms doesn't work as well as undamaged muscle tissue, it takes weeks to heal, and the muscle is weakened and prone to reinjury. A little pain from heavily exercised muscles the morning after an unaccustomed workout is to be expected—but a lot of pain is a signal you're exercising too much, too fast. To prevent muscle pulls, warm up before exercising, then stretch, and stretch again afterwards. The discomfort of mild pulls can be eased by soaking in a hot—but not too hot—bathtub or hot tub. Keep the water about 102 degrees.
- *Shinsplints*, the bane of overactive runners, result from inflammation and injury of the muscles in the front of the lower leg. To avoid them, use top-quality, well-fitting shoes; work up your daily distance

slowly; don't "run through" any pain; stay off concrete and other hard surfaces when running; and try landing on the heel of your foot first, then rocking forward.

DIET

Folk wisdom—and beef industry advertisements—tell us that red meat gives us strength and energy. For decades an extract of beef called beef tea was popular for its healthful effects.

Beef is a good source of protein, needed for healthy muscles, but so is fish, chicken and a well-balanced vegetarian diet. One thing beef has more of than these other protein sources is saturated fat—an item to avoid (see Chapter 14). Another is *carnitine*, an amino acid found in quantity in red meat. Our bodies need carnitine to transport fat inside cells for burning, and the substance has become a popular dietary supplement in recent years, especially among vegetarians.

But it's doubtful that we need any extra carnitine, because our bodies are capable of making all we need from other amino acids present in any well-rounded diet. There is no proof that carnitine supplements build muscle or boost energy. And supplements can be dangerous: Most brands sold are a mixture of two types, D and L. The L form is used by the body; the D form can be toxic.

Muscles are easy to keep healthy with proper nutrition. All they ask for are adequate—not megadose—quantities of some common vitamins and minerals.

MUSCLE FOOD

Keeping muscles healthy and strong isn't hard. Any well-rounded diet with adequate protein (about half that found in the typical American diet) should do the trick. And be sure not to short yourself on the following:

- *Iron* deficiencies, even those that aren't severe enough to cause anemia, can lower muscular performance.
- *Calcium* can help prevent muscle cramps.
- *Potassium* and *magnesium* shortages can lead to tremors.

- *Vitamin B6* has been shown to increase stamina in rats, and is essential in the body's synthesis of carnitine.
- *Vitamin C* is also needed in carnitine production, and muscle weakness is one of the first signs of a C deficiency.
- *Vitamin E*, although it doesn't appear to be a major factor in increasing athletic performance, is effective in treating cramps.

WHAT TO AVOID

If eating red meat was the worst thing people did to build muscle, there would be little cause for worry. But modern science offers us at least three bodybuilding "aids" that range from useless to dangerous.

1. *Electrical stimulation* of muscle recently received media attention as a sweat-free way to keep toned. The laid-back recipient receives small electric shocks that cause muscles to twitch, the theory being that a twitched muscle is as good as an exercised muscle. Not only is the treatment expensive and uncomfortable, but it provides no aerobic, power, skill or stamina benefits.

2. *Steroids* are a group of hormones used to make heftier cattle—and, recently, heftier athletes. The increasing use of steroids by recreational weight lifters and young athletes is a growing problem. The jury is out on whether steroids actually build muscle, but it's in on some of the dangerous side effects: a lowered ability to clear cholesterol out of the bloodstream, a change in sex drive, increased acne, a tendency toward baldness, and an increased risk of liver cancer. Steer clear.

3. *Human growth hormone* (GH) is the latest fad chemical for those who believe bigger is better. It is naturally secreted during childhood to spur body growth, and a lack of it can cause dwarfism. One of the first of the human hormones to be mass-produced by means of genetic engineering, GH is now available to physicians, and many experts are worried about how it will be used. There is little to stop a parent who wants to grow a football player or seven-foot basketball star. There is some evidence that full-grown athletes may be taking GH to increase muscle mass, although there are no good studies on its effects or long-term risks. Until more is known about growth hormone, avoid it.

Part V
INSIDE THE BODY

13

The Brain

You are now engaged in a mystery. Your eyes sense patterns of light reflected off this page. Images of these patterns race to the brain and trigger delicate electroneural storms involving millions of nerve cells. Somehow your brain transforms these purely physical responses into something totally different: thought. No one knows how. The manner in which the brain *thinks* is one of the great puzzles in science.

The mystery of thinking has slowed our understanding of how the brain ages. Without knowing how this complex electrochemical system works in some very basic ways, researchers have difficulty accurately gauging the effects of time on our minds.

But what little is known is encouraging. Despite the physical changes that occur with age—the brain shrinks and nerve cells alter shape—normal aging does not inevitably make you fearful, forgetful and feebleminded. Instead, most people's minds can stay almost as active, flexible and vital at the end of life as in youth. And in some ways the mind gets even better. Because of the large store of experiences that accrue with age, later life can be the richest time for our minds.

Unfortunately, that's not true for everyone. About one older American in ten will suffer from debilitating brain diseases called dementias, which include Alzheimer's disease. This is the "senility" many people fear. But dementias, like so many of the negative stereotypes of the elderly, are not the result of normal aging. They are diseases, preventable in some cases, treatable in others.

NORMAL AGING

Physical Changes

The mature human brain, a three-pound lump of gray and white tissue with the look and consistency of curdled pudding, is fired by about one trillion nerve cells called neurons. Each neuron connects some 50,000 different ways to neighboring neurons, creating a fantastically complex, three-dimensional network.

At birth, the brain is about one-third its full size. Nerve cells multiply rapidly through the first years of life until the brain reaches its full size at about age 20. After this point, growth stops. Through most of our lives, we are unable to grow a single new brain cell.

That would be fine if brain cells never died, but they do—by the millions. A commonly quoted figure is that adults lose 100,000 brain cells each day, and while that may be true on the average, recent research has shown that's a bit simplistic. We now know that rather than shrinking at a constant rate, the brain remains fairly constant in size throughout midlife, then begins a period of relatively rapid shrinkage after age 60. Nerve-cell loss isn't the same everywhere in the brain; by age 90, certain areas may lose up to half their neurons, while others lose practically none.

Older brains are measurably smaller, but researchers disagree as to *how much* they shrink. One research group found that the brain of an average 90-year-old weighed roughly the same as a three-year-old's—about 20 percent less than full-size. Another group found only an average 7-percent change over life, and warned that much of that result might be explained by the fact that the brains of bigger, better-fed young people were compared to smaller oldsters whose nutrition may not have been as good throughout life.

The blood flow to older brains is diminished, and some studies indicate that they use oxygen less efficiently. In addition, individual neurons change with time:

- Older brain cells alter their shape, losing many of the branches that connect them to other brain cells.
- A gummy, age-related pigment called lipofuscin can collect in brain cells, possibly affecting function.
- The slow accumulation of clumps of fibers (called neurofibrillary tangles) is standard inside aging brain cells.

- Concentrations of chemicals that help communication between neurons decline in many regions of the brain.
- There is some evidence that neurons transmit messages a bit more slowly with age.

It's only a small step to assume that these physical changes—shrinking brains, altered neurons—would lead to similar mental changes. A smaller brain that sends messages more slowly fits with the stereotype of feebleminded older people. Luckily, the relationship between physical and mental changes is not that simple.

Very recently, researchers have compared the way older and younger brains burn sugar as they're working. The test gives an indication of how healthy the overall metabolism of the brain is. To their surprise, the results indicated that the brains of healthy aged subjects were just as active and efficient as those of younger people. They concluded that the developing human brain may acquire more cells than it will ever need, leaving plenty after normal aging to support normal function. Their results fit with what is known about mental functioning in normal aging.

Mental Changes

There is no reason to expect a life-altering general mental decline as we grow older. Indeed intelligence tests have shown that most people retain their mental prowess, and some even improve their intelligence scores with advancing age. The physical process of aging, psychologists now believe, is relatively unimportant compared to the individual effects that education and culture exert on our mental state as we grow older. More good news: Most measurable changes in mental ability that do occur with age don't happen until very late in life. During the long stretch from ages 30 to 60, brainpower stays at its peak.

But mental ability involves more than a simple IQ test can show. Brainpower involves the interplay of many processes, measured many ways. A survey of some of the most important factors involved shows both the good and the bad of the aging mind.

Reaction time

One of the simplest tests of mind/body sharpness involves measuring the time it takes people to respond to a stimulus. Until recently, the findings here were thought to be straightforward: With increasing age, reaction times seemed to slow down. Just how much was highly individual. Researchers measured differences of 20 percent in the reaction times of older and younger subjects in some cases, almost nothing in others. In general, the more complex the tasks involved, the greater the differences.

But more recent research underlined the shortcomings of trying to measure real-world skills in the laboratory—and showed that experience balanced much of the slowing in reaction time. Researchers at the University of Wisconsin measured reaction times in tests that simulated real jobs. Although older subjects had more trouble quickly responding to *new* situations than their younger counterparts, both groups were equally capable of speeding up their reactions to *familiar*, already learned stimuli. The key was taking advantage of the accumulated experience of the older subjects in a setting that simulated a real job.

Learning

Tests show that it also takes longer to learn new things as we grow older. But again, researchers can't agree whether that's due to a physical slowing of the brain or simply a deterioration of the skills we employ to help us learn.

Some researchers now believe that what we think of as "intelligence" has less to do with inborn mental power than with the tricks we use to learn. Learning involves strategies and skills that we hone in school and use throughout life. Or at least we should. When was the last time you studied a book as if you were going to be tested on it? If these strategies are allowed to fall by the wayside—if we stop practicing our learning skills—we can lose the ability to learn effectively.

THE PQRST METHOD

This is only one of dozens of strategies developed to make learning easier and memory more effective, but it's a good one to use when reading:

- *Preview* the material you're about to learn and identify the main points.

- *Questions* should be developed that specify what you want to learn from the text.
- *Read* the material carefully, looking for answers to your questions, rereading parts until you feel you've mastered it.
- *State* or repeat the basic points, the central ideas of the reading.
- *Test* yourself by trying to answer the questions you developed to guide your learning.

The PQRST system forces you to do two important things: focus your attention, and organize your thoughts—in this case around the questions you've posed.

The inability to shut out distractions also hinders older people's learning. Researchers have found that the older a person is, the harder it is to pay attention. While it may have been easy in our teens to study while listening to music, it won't be so easy in later years.

But nothing could be farther from the truth than the old saw, "You can't teach an old dog new tricks." Although it may take a little longer, older people who develop effective learning skills and keep them sharp throughout life can continue learning just as well as their younger counterparts.

And they use what they learn. Recent studies have shown that rather than being inflexible and set in their ways, most older people constantly change their habits of dealing with the world in order to cope with stress.

Creativity

Although research in this area is skimpy, we need only look around us to see that creative people can stay creative throughout life. Franz Josef Haydn wrote his finest chamber music after age 65. The renowned photographer Imogen Cunningham is still working in her 90s. Helen Hays stopped wowing them on Broadway long enough to star in a television series in her 70s. Two-time Nobel Prize-winning chemist Linus Pauling lectures and researches into his 80s. Writer Isaac Bashevis Singer is still producing a wealth of stories and books at age 82. And Picasso painted and sculpted after age 90. Although failing eyes, diminished energy or trembling hands may cut back the output, age does not extinguish the creative fire.

Memory

Think you'll lose your memory as you grow older? Forget it! The evidence says that aging does not mean a dramatic decline in memory power—unless you help it happen by letting your mind go.

That's not to say that memory doesn't change throughout life. Researchers divide memory into categories based on the length of time memories are stored. One system divides it up as *short-term* (less than one minute; remembering a telephone number while you dial, for instance), *long-term* (over a period of years) and *very long-term* memory (over a lifetime).

Short-term memory isn't mastered until about age seven, but after that, the evidence shows that you never lose it. There's no reason you shouldn't look up a number and dial the phone as well at 80 as at 18.

Long-term memory involves more effort and skill and changes more through life. It's not until the early teens that most people develop a mature long-term memory. Researchers think it takes that long because long-term memory requires the development of several different skills.

First, of course, we must get the information into our heads. That means learning, and learning strategies can get rusty without constant use. It makes sense that high school and college students, who are forced to repeatedly exercise their long-term memory abilities (or at least long-term enough to get them through a final exam), usually do well on memory tests. The longer you stay in school, the more chance you get to polish your learning skills, so it's no wonder that psychologists have found that more highly educated people have more effective memory skills throughout life. But education alone isn't enough. Although older people in general learn somewhat more slowly than they did when younger, there is a dramatic difference between those who stay intellectually active—reading, discussing, taking classes, *thinking*—and those who don't. Giving the brain a daily workout is just as important as exercising your muscles. Brainwork keeps your learning strategies in shape—and that helps your memory to function at full capacity.

The next part of a healthy long-term memory is retention—the ability to store what you've learned. Memory researchers still don't know whether memories are *lost*—they still exist in the brain, but our mental searching can't turn them up—or *obliterated* entirely as our brain ages. Until more is learned about the chemistry and biology of retention, there is little researchers can recommend.

The third necessity for memory is recall—the ability to bring to mind the memories we've stored. Again, while aging has widely different effects on the recall abilities of different people, research indicates that the older we get, the longer it takes to recall facts. But slower recall is still recall. In fact, aging doesn't seem to have any effect at all on *forgetting*, which takes place at the same rate in younger and older people. The facts are there: It just requires a few more tricks and a bit more time to bring them to mind. Recalling facts is another skill that can be learned and kept in shape with some simple tricks.

ON THE TIP OF YOUR TONGUE

How many times have you had something on the tip of your tongue? You know it's there—you've learned the fact—but you can't quite bring it to mind. The problem is recall. Here are three quick tricks to help you recall:

1. Try to recreate the conditions under which you learned the fact. Remember how that certain song on the radio brings back a flood of memories? Things you learn are bound together with the place, the time, the mood in which you learned them. If you can recreate those conditions in your mind, your recall will improve.

2. Think about related terms or concepts. Sometimes looking for information by asking yourself the same mental question repeatedly can block your recall abilities. Approaching the question from the side, by thinking about related items or questions, can unfreeze the machinery. Say you're trying to remember the name of a movie. Try remembering the name of the leading actor, the theater you saw it in, the people you were with.

3. Go through the alphabet. Running across the first letter of an item can often trigger a memory.

While long-term memory slows with age, very long-term memory does not. This is the cumulative, lifelong storage of experience: early memories, work skills, language, world knowledge and what psychologists call "overlearned skills" such as piano playing and bike riding. The integrity of very long-term memory gives older people an advantage. As experiences and skills accumulate—a process that should continue throughout life—very long-term memories go on developing and growing richer.

The result, if the brain is kept active, can be what was once called the wisdom of old age. Another way researchers look at it is in terms of "fluid" and "crystallized" abilities. Fluid abilities are those that involve abstract thinking, reasoning and adaptation to new situations. The speed and extent of these abilities appear to decline somewhat with age.

But crystallized abilities are made of aggregate experience—the very long-term memories described above. And the growing store of crystallized abilities over time can help offset losses in the fluid department. Consider the difference between a young chess whiz and an old chess master: The younger player speedily analyzes scores of potential moves from a number of angles, many of which are unlikely; the master thinks more slowly but knows from experience how to pare down the possible moves to the few most likely to succeed. The younger player may think *faster*; the older player has learned to think *better*.

So why, if most of the age-related deficits in memory are correctable or minor, do many older people believe they suffer from absentmindedness and memory loss? Part of the answer may lie in the rest of the body. The poor general health suffered by many older people can lower their memory power, as can the heavy use of medicines and drugs so common among older Americans. Brain diseases such as Alzheimer's and other dementias can erase memories in a fraction of older people.

But memory researchers have pinpointed what appear to be even more pervasive, more important factors: self-concept and depression. Simply believing that growing older goes hand-in-hand with a loss of mental abilities can increase anxiety, sap self-confidence and lead to a withdrawal from intellectual life. The result can be memory problems. Depression is common among older Americans and in severe cases can cause what physicians call "pseudodementia," a condition that can include a dramatic—and treatable—loss of memory.

To counter that, think of the mind as a muscle that must be exercised to retain its flexibility and strength. Give it a daily workout. If you reject stereotypes of old age and polish a few simple skills, memory and mind power will stay with you until the day you die.

AGE-RELATED DISEASES

Although normal aging doesn't rob us of our wits, a fraction of older people can fall prey to a variety of diseases that can affect mental functioning. After age 65, about one person in ten will suffer from a physical brain disease—most likely one of the dementias such as Alzheimer's—and about one person in seven will develop some form of mild to severe psychological problem, ranging from depression and anxiety to neurosis and psychosis.

Physical Disease

Alzheimer's, the most feared and best-known type of physical brain disorder, is the disease of the decade. It sometimes seems Alzheimer's has sprung from nowhere to attack hundreds of thousands of Americans. The media keep us up-to-date on the victims: Rita Hayworth has it. Norman Rockwell and Ross MacDonald died from it.

But Alzheimer's is nothing new. The brain lesions typical of the disease were first identified just after the turn of the century by the German neurologist whose name it bears. But Alzheimer's has always been around, usually under the less precise names of presenile or senile dementia. Today it affects between one and two million Americans, and is the fourth or fifth leading cause of death in the United States.

Alzheimer's starts with mild memory loss and personality changes, progresses to confusion, disorientation and violent mood swings, the loss of ability to walk and talk, and finally death. Although it occasionally attacks people in their forties and fifties, Alzheimer's is not a serious problem until later in life, when moderate to severe cases affect between four and five percent of those over 65, climbing to 10 or 12 percent after age 75. Mild cases add another 10 percent to those figures.

There is no known cause of the disease, no prevention and no cure. Scientists are looking at a variety of possible causes including genetic links, autoimmunity (the body's immune system reacting against something in the brain), changes in hormone levels, toxins, environmental agents like aluminum, and even viruses.

Some researchers believe Alzheimer's is a speeding up of the normal changes that affect everyone's neurons—a sort of accelerated aging of the brain. They point out that many of the features that mark the brain of Alzheimer's patients are also hallmarks of normal aging, such as the clumps of fibers inside neurons mentioned earlier. They hypothesize that this revving up of the aging process may be kicked off by a toxin or virus.

So much attention has been focused on Alzheimer's that it is easy to forget that it is responsible for only about half of the senile dementias in the United States.

The second most common physical brain disease, multi-infarct dementia, is caused when blocked blood vessels cut off the blood supply to small areas of the brain, killing the neurons in those area. Multi-infarct dementia is tied to high blood pressure and is in many cases preventable or treatable.

Fear of Alzheimer's has caused many older persons to suffer un-necessarily when they notice one or more of the symptoms associated with the disease: loss of memory, disorientation, inability to express oneself, personality changes. Not only can these symptoms be caused by a potentially treatable brain disease, like multi-infarct dementia, but they may also be caused by things as simple and correctable as fatigue, overmedication, drinking, malnutrition or depression.

Psychological Disorders

Depression is by far the most common complaint encountered by psychologists who specialize in treating the elderly. That's not surprising. Depression is the number-one psychological complaint among all age groups, and is no more common among the elderly than among the young. However, increasing age can deepen the blues by adding new crises to cope with: the loss of friends, scattering of family and worsening general health. The problem is aggravated by a society that places no premium on old age, pays older people little attention, gives them little respect and robs them of worthwhile activity.

Again, self-concept plays an important role. Allowing yourself to believe that old age inevitably means a loss of dignity and ability is the straightest road to depression. Allowing yourself to fall prey to the stereotypes of old age—introversion, crankiness, inflexibility—makes depression more likely.

But the facts show that none of these stereotypical changes happen with increasing age. Instead, psychologists have found, your individual personality is set by young adulthood and remains relatively stable throughout life. There is no such thing as a "typical" older person. Individual personality differences among persons of all ages are much more pronounced than the effects of age itself.

TOWARD A HAPPIER OLD AGE

Whenever researchers conduct large-scale psychological studies on older people, they find a special group. These are older people that don't seem to have aged. They are relatively free of physical and mental problems, have solid relationships and high activity levels, are outgoing and shrewd, well-adjusted and happy. They tend to live longer than others. About one person in seven over the age of 65 falls into this group.

They're sometimes called "supernormals," and they somehow have found the key to a happier old age. Although no single factor has been discovered to account for their aging success, supernormals often have these things in common:

- They tend to be well-educated or come from high-level, high-responsibility jobs.
- They tend to be extroverted and remain socially active.
- Their attitudes toward leisure activities, security, health and friendships are the same as those of younger people.
- They have strong feelings of being useful.

Supernormals may also be genetically blessed. They have better overall health than most of their peers, which helps them avoid the pain and medications that can affect the functioning of older people.

But the important factors appear to be things that are somewhat under their control—habits that were cultivated and maintained throughout life. Supernormals start out mentally active, often attaining a high level of formal education, often taking on high-powered jobs. After retirement, they stay intellectually active and involved.

Keeping up a high level of activity, not surprisingly, is also the advice psychologists give people to fight depression. A lifelong interest and participation in education, as we've seen, keeps memory and learning skills in shape, which in turn make it possible to enjoy new ideas. A job with responsibility and rewards gives supernormals a feeling of usefulness, and working part-time, whether volunteer or paid, keeps that feeling alive.

14

Heart and Lungs

Forget heartaches, heartthrobs and wearing your heart on your sleeve. Forget kind, breaking, broken and bleeding hearts. Shaped more like a blunt cone than a box of Valentine's Day candy, the heart has nothing to do with love, but everything to do with life. Its beat is the sound of our survival.

Every day the heart pumps almost 2,000 gallons of blood through more than 60,000 miles of blood vessels. This tireless muscle, only fist-sized and a mere half pound, beats 3.2 billion times during an 80-year lifetime. On either side of the heart, the lungs, with their 200 square feet of surface, inflate more than 23,000 times a day, trapping air in some 300 million tiny sacs.

Think of the heart as a four-chambered, electrically powered machine hooked into a vast network of tubing—arteries to carry blood to the cells of the body, veins to carry blood back to the heart. Used, oxygen-depleted blood is whisked to the heart's upper right chamber. Fresh, oxygen-rich blood from the lungs pours into the upper left chamber. Like clockwork, an electrical impulse causes the two upper chambers to contract. The valves between upper and lower chambers open and blood rushes into the two lower chambers. Another electrical impulse causes the lower chambers to squeeze, forcing the fresh blood out through the arteries and throughout the body. The used blood rushes to the lungs where, across millions of cell walls thinner than the surface of soap bubbles, carbon dioxide is swapped for oxygen. Now rejuvenated, the blood travels back to the heart, where the cycle begins again.

This is the unremitting routine of pump and bellows as they toil in tandem to nourish the cells of the body. This is a strong heart and healthy lungs at work. But all may not go so smoothly when a combination of bad habits, inactivity and age takes its toll.

WHAT CAN HAPPEN TO THE HEART, BLOOD VESSELS AND LUNGS

Leonardo da Vinci was sure he knew what caused aging: "veins which by the thickening of their tunics in the old restrict the passage of blood, and by this lack of nourishment destroy life . . ." He was on the right track. Today's researchers believe that most harmful changes in the cardiovascular system are the result of stiffened blood vessels and heart muscle. And they think, just as da Vinci theorized almost five centuries ago, that a weakened cardiovascular system may underlie much of the general physical decline in the elderly.

Exactly what happens to our heart, blood vessels and lungs as we age? Scientists are not really sure they know. Their studies show that the cardiovascular and respiratory systems decline in function and efficiency as we grow older. But are these changes a natural consequence of the aging process or the result of years of bad habits? The line between normal aging and self-imposed decline is fuzzy. This is what the research shows:

- The heart becomes less muscular and more full of useless, inelastic tissue. This stiffening decreases the heart's ability to contract, and its pumping efficiency suffers. The heart takes longer to expel blood, leaving less time for filling.
- The heart's lack of elasticity combined with the progressive stiffness and narrowing of large arteries reduce the blood's circulation throughout the body.
- Stiffness throughout the cardiovascular system leads to an increase in blood pressure.
- The heart pumps less blood with each beat, especially during exercise. Thirty years ago, scientists believed that the volume of blood pumped decreased five percent from age 30 to 40, another five percent from 40 to 50 and almost ten percent from 50 to 60. Now these statistics are seriously being questioned.

- The heart becomes more sluggish in its response to stress. When faced with increased work load (exercise), heart rate does not increase as it once did.
- The airways and tissues of the lungs, including the air sacs, become less elastic and more rigid, making the whole respiratory tract less efficient.
- The amount of air that can be brought into the lungs with the deepest possible breath declines steadily after age 30. At 70 it is half the volume it was at 30.
- The body's maximum intake of oxygen during rigorous exercise (known as VO_2 max) declines about one percent a year beginning in the 30s.

VARICOSE VEINS

Never underestimate the power of gravity. The body's architect did—and the result is varicose veins.

According to nature's logic, veins are constructed of less sturdy stuff than arteries. They don't have to be as tough because the blood they carry, unlike arterial blood, is not under strong pumping pressure from the heart. The problem is that blood pressure in veins, especially in the legs, is so weak that it's barely enough to balance the downward tug of gravity. To compensate, many veins contain one-way valves designed to prevent backflow. But sometimes gravity wins.

Prolonged standing, protracted sitting (especially with crossed legs) and excess weight all put increased pressure on leg veins. Pregnancy not only adds weight but also releases hormones that tend to relax vein walls. Heredity can be an enemy too. Some people apparently inherit weak valves and vein walls.

Whatever the cause, a vein sometimes succumbs. Its wall bulges, its valves no longer close properly and gravity prevents the normal return of blood to the heart. This blood accumulates in pools, which stretch the veins even more and make the valves less effective.

The result is the bulging, bluish, all-too-visible ropes running down the legs. The bad news is that once you have varicose veins, you have them for life—unless you subject yourself to painful, expensive and sometimes not altogether successful "vein stripping" surgery. The good news is that those not genetically doomed can do several things to prevent varicose veins from ever occurring:

- Keep your weight down.
- Exercise regularly to increase circulation.
- Elevate your feet whenever possible.
- Wear support hose to help counter gravity.

At best, these changes slow us down; at worst, they kill us. Heart disease—often the result of stiffened, narrowed arteries and scarred, inelastic heart tissue—is this country's number one killer, accounting for more than half of all deaths. A million and a half people suffer heart attacks each year. More than half a million die from them. Men are especially susceptible, and although the incidence of heart disease has decreased dramatically during the past decade, still, one man in five has a heart attack before age 60.

WOMEN AND HEART DISEASE

If you think only middle-aged men need worry about heart disease, think again. It's true that a woman of any age runs a significantly lower risk of suffering from coronary ailments than a man of the same age. But heart disease is the number-one killer of both men *and* women in the United States today. What should women be particularly concerned about? Here's what recent research has shown:

- Women who take contraceptive pills and also smoke increase their risk of heart attack tenfold.
- Women older than 40 who take the Pill run five times the risk of suffering a heart attack.
- Postmenopausal women are at increased risk compared with premenopausal women.
- Removal of a woman's ovaries prior to natural menopause appears to put her at increased risk.

- Almost two and a half times as many women as men suffer second heart attacks within six years. (This may be because women tend to have heart attacks at an older age than men.)
- Women are more likely to die from a heart attack than men. (Again, it may be because women are older at the time of attack.)
- Middle-aged women have not experienced the same recent decline in death from heart disease as men of the same age.

Is the progressive decline that leads to heart disease inevitable? Yes, say some scientists who insist that the cardiovascular system was not designed for long life. The heart is rich in tissue that naturally loses its elasticity, they point out. Artery walls are not particularly well-supplied with blood. The entire system is subject to continuous, severe mechanical stress. Their ideas are buttressed by numerous studies that show declining efficiency of the heart, blood vessels and lungs.

But this view is now being challenged. Today, many scientists argue that the earlier studies showing cardiovascular decline were done on sickly and sedentary older people whose bodies reflected disease and disuse, not normal aging. Newer research, they say, suggests that much of the decline in the capacity and efficiency of heart and lungs may be the result of inactivity, diet, smoking and stress.

In fact, age itself may be only one of many risk factors that lead to "aging" and ailing hearts, blood vessels and lungs. If this is true—and the evidence is mounting that it is—then we can actually stave off much of this not-inevitable decline. The key is recognizing the major risk factors and making positive changes in our life-style now, before the damage is done.

WHAT ARE THE RISK FACTORS?

People age at different rates. That's as true for the visible signs of aging like gray hair and wrinkles as it is for the invisible changes like clogged arteries and a weakened heart. What makes one person's cardiovascular system strong and efficient at age 60 while another person slows down at 40? Researchers have found that a number of factors can increase the risk of falling prey to an ailing heart.

A few risk factors are beyond our control: *gender* (men are at higher risk than women), *family history* (there may be an inherited tendency toward heart disease), *diabetes* (diabetics are more prone to build-ups of fatty deposits in the arteries) and *age* (those over 55 are more susceptible). But we can control the other risk factors. And if we do, studies show that we can significantly reduce our chances of succumbing to heart disease. How many of the following self-imposed risks are you running?

Poor Diet

The dirty word of the decade is cholesterol. But this waxy, yellow fat found in food and made in the body is not nearly as villainous as you may think. Cholesterol helps the body produce bile and is needed for the manufacture of vitamin D and some hormones, including sex hormones. It is part of the essential coating that provides strength and protection to cells and nerves. In other words, some cholesterol in the blood is vital for a healthy body. That's why the liver manufactures enough of it to supply all the body's cholesterol needs.

The problem is not cholesterol but *excess* cholesterol, which many scientists believe to be the leading risk factor in heart disease. In Japan, where smoking is as common as in the United States and where high blood pressure is as frequent, there are one-eighth to one-tenth the number of heart attacks. Why? One explanation is that Japanese tend to have much lower concentrations of cholesterol in their blood than Americans. Diet makes the difference.

Nutritionists estimate that fat accounts for more than 40 percent of the calories in the average American diet. And much of that fat—from animal sources like eggs, dairy foods and meat—is saturated and cholesterol-rich. Cholesterol in food (dietary cholesterol) and cholesterol in the blood (serum cholesterol) are not the same, but researchers now believe that increases in the first lead to increases in the second.

How much cholesterol in the blood is too much? Until a few years ago, most physicians and scientists were saying that those over 40 with serum cholesterol counts above 240—about 20 percent of Americans—ran an increased risk of premature heart disease. But more recent studies have made the medical community even more cautious. A panel of experts meeting at the National Institutes of Health in December 1984 concluded that levels above 200 to 230—this would include a staggering 50 percent of the U.S. adult population—are associated with increased risk. A simple, inexpensive blood test can measure your cholesterol level.

Why is excess cholesterol in the blood so harmful? The fatty substance coats blood vessels, inhibiting oxygen exchange. It forms deposits that line the arteries, restricting—and, over time, sometimes completely blocking—the passage of blood. Cholesterol-clogged arteries (atherosclerosis) can lead to a heart attack if a coronary artery is blocked or to a stroke if an artery serving the brain is clogged.

Although an estimated half of all Americans show signs of atherosclerosis when they die, the condition is not a disease of old age. In fact, for the average American, cholesterol deposits in the arteries begin early in life. Autopsy studies of U.S. GIs killed in the Korean War (who presumably grew up eating the typical American fat-saturated diet) showed that more than 75 percent had cholesterol deposits. Their average age? Twenty-two. Additional proof of the cholesterol/heart disease link comes from a recently completed, ten-year, $150 million study. Results from the National Heart, Lung and Blood Institute study suggest that for every 1-percent reduction in serum cholesterol there is a 2-percent reduction in coronary heart disease.

Fat is our major dietary problem, but it's not our only one. Americans also consume far too much sodium—as much as 60 times more than the body needs—which can make blood pressure soar. Table salt, about 40 percent sodium, is the biggest culprit. A mere tenth of a teaspoon provides us with all the sodium our bodies need. Canned vegetables, highly processed convenience foods and cured meats may also be loaded with sodium. Sources include these ingredients commonly found in prepared foods: monosodium glutamate (msg), sodium benzoate, sodium saccharin or sodium nitrite.

The average American diet is also high in refined sugar, which elevates fatty substances in blood, encourages obesity and intensifies the effects of excess sodium. Alcohol and caffeine—the all-American drugs—may spell trouble too. In large amounts, alcohol contributes to weight problems and may raise blood pressure and cause cardiac muscle damage. Caffeine's effect is still controversial, but some research indicates that it too helps elevate blood pressure.

Smoking

In the face of increasingly damning Surgeon General reports and forceful anti-tobacco media campaigns, even devoted smokers now realize their addiction can have severe, widespread health effects—especially on the lungs and heart.

During the past few decades, researchers have established an incontrovertible link between smoking and lung cancer. The Surgeon General now estimates that smoking contributes to 85 percent of the approximately 130,000 lung cancer deaths each year. Other figures suggest that 90 percent of all lung cancer occurs in people who smoke. Scientists also note the parallel rise in the number of female cigarette smokers and lung cancer deaths among women since World War II. Lung cancer is now the number one cancer killer among women, with cases and deaths currently increasing by about seven percent a year.

Cigarettes also wreak havoc on the cardiovascular system. In fact, about half of the 350,000 deaths attributable to smoking each year come from heart attacks. The relative risk of heart attack due to smoking appears to be greatest for men in their 30s and 40s. Population studies show that smokers have a 70 percent greater risk of dying from a heart attack than nonsmokers. Two-pack-a-dayers increase their risk 200 percent.

Smoking increases hardening and narrowing of the arteries. Nicotine in cigarettes and carbon monoxide in smoke may injure the cells that line blood vessels, causing an increase in fat deposits and a gradual narrowing. Substances in tobacco also thicken and increase the stickiness of blood, making clotting a potential problem. Nicotine constricts blood vessels and raises blood pressure. Carbon monoxide restricts the amount of oxygen carried in the blood.

"Type A" Behavior

Are you impatient, hard-driving and competitive? Do you eat, talk and drive fast? Feel constantly pressured? Have a difficult time relaxing? If so, you're exhibiting classic "Type A" behavior, and research shows you may be two to three times more likely to suffer a heart attack than your relaxed "Type B" counterpart. Dr. Meyer Friedman, the San Francisco cardiologist who first identified these personality types in 1959, estimates that as many as three-quarters of urban males exhibit some Type A behavior. His colleague, Stanford researcher Dr. Carl Thoresen, says women are suffering increasingly from chronic stress. Those most at risk are highly competitive young career women. Do you recognize any of these traits in yourself?

- Thinking of or doing two or more things simultaneously.
- Scheduling more and more activities into less and less time.
- Interrupting others when they speak.
- Becoming unduly irritated when forced to wait in line or stop for a red light.
- Playing nearly every game to win, even when playing with children.
- Making a fetish of always being on time.

Type A behavior seems to make people particularly susceptible to heart attacks, angina and coronary heart disease because they keep their personal stress levels high. In fact, they encounter stress in everything they do, responding to challenges as if they were full-scale emergencies. This hyper response triggers excess secretions of three hormones, two of which are known to damage arteries.

Stress

Stress itself isn't bad—life without a certain amount of tension would be boring—it's how we deal with it. Those exhibiting Type A behavior become impatient, hostile and frustrated. Others may internalize stress or respond to it by smoking or overeating. In the absence of positive responses like exercise, meditation or other stress-control techniques, stress can be a definite risk factor in coronary heart disease.

Inactivity

The less active we are, the less healthy we tend to be. Lack of regular, vigorous exercise can easily translate into extra pounds that strain the entire cardiovascular system. Without frequent workouts, muscles—be they bicep or cardiac—lose their tone and become less efficient. Inactivity leads to below par overall fitness, which can mean poor response to stress and sluggish recovery from sudden exertion.

Specifically, inactivity increases the risk of heart disease and may even shorten life. In one of the most important studies of the relationship between exercise and health, Stanford researcher Ralph Paffenbarger, Jr. found that men who burned fewer than 2,000 calories a week by exercising had a 64 percent higher risk of heart attack than their more active counterparts. The same study found that the risk of death from both coronary heart disease and respiratory illness was highest for the least active men.

Excess Weight

Extra pounds tax both the heart and lungs, making them work harder to achieve the same results. Excess weight can affect the blood vessels, contributing to elevated blood pressure and varicose veins. Obesity is also associated with high blood-cholesterol levels and diabetes.

But it's not just weight, it's where we carry it. Swedish researchers found that men and women who carry their weight in their waists rather than their hips had three to five times the incidence of heart attacks and strokes. Apparently fat cells in the abdomen are more likely than other fat cells to release fatty acids into the blood. This may be one reason why women, who tend to carry their excess weight around their hips, suffer fewer heart attacks than men.

High Blood Pressure (Hypertension)

Dubbed "the silent killer," high blood pressure affects an estimated 60 million American adults, including 40 percent of retirement-age whites and 50 percent of retirement-age blacks. Most often symptomless, it ultimately causes irreversible damage to the cardiovascular system. When blood courses through an artery with excessive force, it can damage the blood vessel's lining and promote cholesterol build-up.

Hypertension greatly increases the risk of strokes, heart attacks and heart failure. One study found that those with high blood pressure ran five times the risk of heart attacks as those with normal pressure. Other research with men age 30-60 found that high blood pressure doubled the likelihood of heart attacks and multiplied the chance of strokes by four.

A blood-pressure reading measures the force of blood against the walls of the arteries. Expressed in two numbers—120/80 is considered an average reading for adults—it measures both maximum pressure when the heart is pumping blood (the first number) and minimum pressure between heart beats (the second number). Repeated measurements in excess of 140/90 indicate hypertension.

No one knows what causes most hypertension, but researchers have pinpointed a number of factors that increase the risk of elevated blood pressure. Not surprisingly, these are the same risk factors as for heart attacks:

- *Excess body weight* imposes an added burden on the heart, forcing it to pump more blood through a larger body. Blood pressure increases correspondingly.
- *Lack of exercise* often translates into weight problems. Even if you can maintain an appropriate weight without regular physical activity, your circulatory system and heart muscle suffer from under-use.
- *Poor diet*, including excess sodium, refined sugar, alcohol and caffeine, may contribute to elevated blood pressure.
- *Smoking* raises blood pressure and constricts arteries.
- *Oral contraceptives* may raise blood pressure and increase the chance of blood clots.
- *Stress*, or rather how you handle it, can also be a factor. Those ex-hibiting "Type A" behavior are prone to high blood pressure.
- *Race* (blacks are more prone to hypertension than whites), *sex* (men are at greater risk than women) and *age* (blood pressure may elevate as we get older) are the only unavoidable risk factors. But researchers now believe that age by itself does not represent a substantial risk.

Although high blood pressure is usually symptomless, it is easily detectable. Doctors recommend yearly blood-pressure checks for those over 30. As yet, there is no cure for most hypertension, but it can be controlled. Many people respond to changes in diet and life-style. Some require drug therapy.

WHAT YOU CAN DO TO KEEP HEART, LUNGS AND BLOOD VESSELS YOUNG AND HEALTHY

"Heart disease before age 80 is our own fault," says pioneer cardiologist and exercise advocate Dr. Paul Dudley White. He may be stretching the point—risk factors like diabetes, gender and race are beyond our control—but he's on the right track. More and more research is showing that age by itself does not cause the "aging" of the cardiovascular system. It is primarily our unhealthy habits and life-styles that are to blame. That means it is within our power to keep our hearts strong, our arteries cholesterol-free and our lungs efficient. How?

Modify Your Diet

Americans eat the wrong foods. The average American diet—larded with fat, brimming with sodium and devoid of fiber—is a clear hazard to the cardiovascular system. Here are the changes nutritionists and researchers suggest:

- *Reduce fat intake.* Americans get 42 percent of their calories from fat. Nutritionists urge lowering that number to 10-15 percent. Concentrate on severely limiting or eliminating saturated fat from your diet. That means cutting consumption of cream, butter, whole milk, eggs, fatty meats and organ meats. Pay attention to the cholesterol content of the foods you eat.

CHOLESTEROL IN COMMON FOODS

Limit cholesterol intake to 250 to 300 mg. a day, say the experts at the American Heart Association. Some nutritionists suggest even lower levels, regardless of your serum cholesterol count or age. To choose a sensible diet, take note of the cholesterol content of these common foods:

Food	Amount	Cholesterol (mgs.)
Whole milk	1 cup	33
Skim milk	1 cup	4
Cheddar cheese	1 oz.	60
Mozzarella cheese	1 oz.	16
Butter	1 tbsp.	31
Margarine	1 tbsp.	0
Broiled white fish	4 oz.	57
Roast chicken	4 oz.	96
Lean pork or ham	4 oz.	100
Lean ground beef	4 oz.	106
Steamed shrimp	4 oz.	234
Large egg	1	274

EIGHT WAYS TO CUT CHOLESTEROL

1. Eat no more than 6 oz. of lean fish, poultry or meat a day, steering clear of organ meats (liver, sweet-breads) and processed meats (salami, bologna) as much as possible.
2. Trim fat from meats and skin poultry before cooking.
3. Bake, broil, steam or roast food. Don't fry it.
4. Avoid foods served or cooked in cream sauces or cheese sauces.
5. Eat no more than three egg yolks a week, including eggs used in cooking.
6. Forget butter. Use vegetable oil when cooking and margarine on the table.
7. Drink and cook with skim milk, not whole milk.
8. Avoid high-fat desserts like cheesecake, ice cream and anything topped with whipped cream.

- *Eat fish.* A superior source of protein, seafood is low in total fat as well as saturated fats. Depending on the species, only 11 to 27 percent of the total fat in seafood is saturated, compared to 36 percent in pork and 48 percent in beef. Even more important are the special cholesterol-fighting oils found in many fish and shellfish. These fish oils may guard against heart attacks and strokes by thinning the blood, making it less viscous and slower to clot. They also seem to sweep out cholesterol by changing the body's blood chemistry. Scientists don't know yet how the mechanism works, but fish oil forces down the levels of what's commonly called "bad cholesterol"—actually not cholesterol at all but the chemical shuttle that carries cholesterol *into* body tissues—while pushing up the concentration of "good cholesterol"—the shuttle that carries cholesterol *away* from body tissues. In a study at Oregon Health Sciences University, average blood-cholesterol levels plummeted 17 percent when subjects ate a diet based on salmon and salmon oil as the only sources of fat.
- *Add other cholesterol-fighting foods to your diet.* Studies at the University of Kentucky show that *oat bran* lowers blood levels of

"bad cholesterol." A half cup of oat bran worked into an otherwise typical American diet lowered levels as much as 25 percent within ten days. Other researchers report that *beans* reduced serum cholesterol by 19 percent and lowered "bad cholesterol" by 23 percent within three weeks. *Onions, garlic* and *yogurt* also appear to inhibit the rise of blood cholesterol. U.S. Department of Agriculture researchers say that the pectin content in *apples* helps lower cholesterol levels by slowing the digestion of cholesterol-rich foods. In animal studies, *eggplant* appears to prevent the build-up of cholesterol in blood vessels by slowing its absorption in the intestines.

- *Increase vitamin C-rich foods or take a vitamin C supplement.* Researchers are finding that vitamin C is a good defense against elevated cholesterol levels, hardened arteries and heart disease. In a British study, elderly patients with coronary problems took one gram of vitamin C (1,000 milligrams or the equivalent of ten cups of orange juice) daily. After six weeks, total blood-cholesterol levels dropped and concentrations of the "good cholesterol" increased.

- *Pay attention to minerals.* In addition to helping curb bone loss, *calcium* may impart some protection against cholesterol-clogged arteries, according to Iowa State researchers. Required for normal rhythmic contractions of the heart muscle and proper blood clotting, calcium also helps reduce the levels of toxins in the blood. *Chromium* lowers both cholesterol and sugar levels in the blood. *Magnesium* is necessary for relaxing heart muscles, and *potassium* maintains heartbeat regularity.

- *Reduce sodium intake.* A high-sodium diet is linked to hypertension. Table salt is a major offender, but merely banishing the saltshaker from the table won't do the trick. Convenience foods, highly processed foods, cured meats and many carbonated drinks can be extraordinarily high in sodium. Read labels carefully.

Stop Smoking

Shaking free of this powerful addiction—some say tobacco is more addictive than heroin—is no easy task. But the benefits are almost immediate. Your body cleanses itself of nicotine within about five days. Your lungs, clogged with tars and other substances, begin to function normally when damaged or destroyed cilia (microscopic hairs that act as cleansing brushes) have a chance to regrow, usually within six months. A year after quitting, you have significantly decreased your cigarette-linked risk of heart disease, and after ten or more smoke-free years, you are statistically at no greater risk than a lifelong nonsmoker. Lung-cancer risks take longer to reduce, but within fifteen years, an ex-smoker's chances of developing the disease are almost as low as a nonsmoker. Yet another benefit: Nonsmokers appear to have higher concentration of the "good cholesterol" in their blood than smokers.

Exercise Regularly

A thrice-weekly program of aerobic exercise can help burn up fatty acids and lower cholesterol. A major study of 17,000 Harvard alumni found that exercise dramatically lowered the risk of heart attack, even

CONDITIONING EXERCISES FOR HEART AND LUNGS

The conditioning power of various activities depends on four things: level of effort expended, duration of the activity, frequency and your current level of conditioning. A healthy, reasonably active person can refer to the table below. But if you are already highly conditioned, doing the exercises in the first column 15 minutes, three times a week probably won't maintain your current level of conditioning, let alone improve it. If, however, you lead an extremely sedentary life-style, as little as five minutes of walking a day will improve cardiovascular conditioning.

Will condition if 15 min., 3 x/wk.	Will condition if brisk, 30 min., 3 x/wk.	Won't condition
x-country skiing	bicycling	bowling
uphill hiking	basketball	football
jumping rope	calisthenics	golf
running	dance	lifting weights
stationary cycling	downhill skiing	softball
	handball	volleyball
	racquetball	
	swimming	
	tennis	
	walking	

among those who had high blood pressure, smoked, were overweight or had parents with heart disease. Switching from a sedentary to an active life-style could cut an average man's heart-attack risk by a third, estimates the director of the study. Exercise works the heart muscle and lungs, enhancing oxygen intake and contributing to overall fitness. A ten-year study at the University of Wisconsin found that intense exercise can prevent the typical ten-percent-per-decade drop in fitness. Need more reasons? Exercise helps reduce stress and lower weight.

Maintain Normal Weight

Overweight people have higher blood pressure, higher cholesterol levels and a greater tendency towards diabetes than their slimmer counterparts. If you cut down on fat in your diet and exercise regularly, you should be able to maintain your optimum weight.

Learn to Cope with Everyday Stress

Whether you're a hard-driving "Type A" or a relaxed "Type B," learning to cope with stress can reduce the risk of heart disease. A six-year study at Stanford found that Type A men and women greatly reduced their chances of suffering a heart attack by modifying their aggressive behavior. After three years of psychological group-counseling to curb excessive Type A traits, the men and women had half as many recurrent attacks as those who hadn't learned to modify their behavior. Other ways of coping with stress include relaxation techniques, yoga, meditation, biofeedback and exercise. But don't take your Type A behavior with you to the gym. A Shippensburg University researcher found that urging yourself faster, harder and further when you exercise raises levels of a stress hormone that can damage the cardiovascular system.

15

Digestion and Diet

It'll be so-long to szechuan and good-bye to gumbo. Curry? A distant memory. Chili? Out of the question. You'll be nibbling at dry toast and cottage cheese, facing breakfasts of stewed prunes, coddled eggs and bran cereal.

If this is what you imagine for you and your stomach's future, you are decidedly and happily wrong. Scientists studying the effect of normal aging on digestion have found only minor changes in the body's ability to digest and absorb nutrients. Sure, some older people have digestive problems. But researchers are finding that these troubles are more often related to poor nutrition, unhealthy eating and drinking habits, lack of exercise and use of medications than they are to normal aging.

SIX MYTHS ABOUT DIGESTION

We're walking encyclopedias of misinformation when it comes to digestion. We latch on to (unwise) folk wisdom and put our faith in (fictitious) scientific "fact." How many of these myths do you still believe?

1. *MYTH*: Lying down after a big meal aids digestion.
    FACT: Lying down after a big meal is one of the best ways to get heartburn.

2. *MYTH:* To calm your stomach or quell an ulcer attack, drink milk. *FACT:* Not only does milk stimulate acid production and thus increase the chance of stomach upset, it is also difficult to digest for some people and can cause a host of unpleasant symptoms from gas to diarrhea.

3. *MYTH:* To settle your stomach, drink a cup of hot tea. *FACT:* Tea and coffee (including decaf) stimulate acid secretion, which can aggravate an already upset stomach or do damage to an ulcer.

4. *MYTH:* People in stressful jobs are most likely to get ulcers. *FACT:* There is no evidence that those in particular occupations or tax brackets have a higher risk of getting ulcers than anyone else.

5. *MYTH:* For a nervous stomach, bowel problems or ulcers, switch to a bland diet. *FACT:* Research shows that a bland diet does not help alleviate digestive problems.

6. *MYTH:* Laxatives are the first line of defense against constipation. *FACT:* Chronic use of laxatives can actually cause constipation. A high-fiber diet is the answer.

WHAT HAPPENS TO OUR DIGESTIVE SYSTEM AS WE AGE?

Every part of the digestive tract changes as we age, but no single change, nor all of them together, drastically affects the system as a whole. Because digestion is essential to life—unlike, say, a full head of hair or 20/20 vision—the system is not only designed to last, it is designed to operate adequately even when its component parts become sluggish.

Here's what happens to our digestive tract as we grow older:

- The *salivary glands* begin producing less saliva with a lower concentration of digestive enzymes. There's no evidence that this affects digestion.

THE DIGESTIVE TRACT

Food takes a 12- to 48-hour trek down the digestive tract. Knowing where it goes and what happens to it can help us keep our systems running smoothly.

- The process begins in the *mouth*, where chewing breaks food into bits and mixes it with enzyme-rich saliva.
- Food moves down the *esophagus*, a foot-long muscular tube that contracts to push food toward the stomach.
- In the *stomach*, food is crushed and combined with digestive juices and enzymes. After four or five hours, it is ready to move on.
- Arriving in the 20-foot-long coil of *small intestine*, food is bathed in a variety of enzymes and juices secreted by the *liver* and *pancreas*. Here food is broken down into simpler nutrients which are absorbed into the bloodstream. After about three hours, all that remains is waste, in the form of indigestible vegetable fiber, bile products, salt and water.
- On its final leg of the journey, waste travels through the *colon* or large intestine at a leisurely pace. It takes from 24 to 48 hours for sufficient water to be absorbed from the waste, making it ready for elimination.

- Food takes longer to make its way down the *esophagus* because of a decrease in the wave-like motion that pushes the food toward the stomach. But this has little apparent effect on digestion. And neither do hiatal hernias—protrusions of the stomach or other structures through the opening in the diaphragm designed for the esophagus. They commonly develop in 40- to 60-year olds, but most are symptomless. Doctors call them "trivial aberrations."
- In the *stomach*, production of gastric juices declines from age 20 on. In the middle years, there's an increased incidence of chronic inflammation of the stomach with degeneration of the mucous lining (known as atrophic gastritis). Either or both of these changes can prevent an older body from absorbing as much iron and vitamin B12 as a younger one. Happily, improved nutrition can take up the slack.

- As we age, food may take a bit longer to travel through the 20-odd feet of the *small intestines*, but researchers have found little evidence that this affects digestion. The lining of the intestine, they say, has an enormous reserve absorptive capacity. But, according to other studies, the intestine does lose some of its ability to adapt to unusual situations like low calcium or high fat intake. Fortunately, this isn't a problem for the nutritionally aware person of any age. One intestinal age-related change that does bother some people is increasing intolerance of milk products when, over time, the enzyme that breaks down milk sugar (lactose) disappears from the intestinal tract.

- The *liver* goes through a number of age-related changes including reduction of enzyme concentrations, but this organ has a startlingly large reserve capacity. Scientists say that 80 percent of the liver can be removed without impairing its function.

- In the *pancreas*, studies show age-related changes in the making and secretion of digestive enzymes, but scientists have discovered no evidence that this affects digestion.

- As we age, we run an increased risk of getting gallstones in the *gallbladder* or bile duct.

- In the large intestine or *colon*, two important changes take place. First, it appears that the muscular walls of the colon weaken with age. Because of this, small pouches (called diverticula) may balloon out from the colon wall. In some people, the pouches become inflamed and infected. Second, the colon's wave-like motion slows down or weakens. This means there's more opportunity for water to be absorbed from the waste, thus increasing the chance of constipation. A high-fiber diet often solves both problems.

Although the list of age-related changes is impressive, scientists stress the amazing reserves of the digestive tract. As two Johns Hopkins School of Medicine researchers put it: "Considerable curtailment of normal function can occur without appreciably affecting measurable physiological processes." Translation: We may still be able to enjoy pepperoni pizza well into old age, even though our gut isn't what it used to be.

But that doesn't mean we can abuse our digestive system — overloading it with fats, depriving it of fiber, dousing it in alcohol — and still expect nature to be kind to us. Digestive problems are all too common, and they tend to become even more common as we age. But in most cases, age is not the villain—life-style is. Whether it's the mild discomfort of an overfull stomach or the wrenching pain of an ulcer, we have control over much of what can go wrong with our digestive tract.

GAS

The subject of many a sophomoric joke, gas is no laughing matter to the sufferer. Although anyone who swallows either air or food—that is, everyone—gets gas, it seems to trouble the young and the aging rather than the in-between. Babies are gas-prone because they swallow air as they drink from bottle or breast. People in their 20s and 30s have problems because of poor eating habits, nervous temperaments and lactose (milk sugar) intolerance.

We may blame those stabbing gas pains on the chili dog we ate for lunch, but doctors say that two-thirds of the gas in most people's systems is simply swallowed air. Fast eaters, straw sippers, cold sufferers and coffee gulpers are good candidates for stomach gas caused by swallowed air. And because some air is swallowed each time saliva goes down, habits that make the mouth water, like chewing gum, smoking and sucking mints, can also cause gas. Carbonated beverages are an obvious hazard.

Should we commit any of those table sins our parents warned us about—talking with a full mouth, chewing with an open mouth, slurping hot soup—our punishment may be painful stomach gas and its socially unacceptable counterpart: the belch. The best defense is a relaxed mealtime atmosphere. Remember that over-the-counter remedies, which may or may not help alleviate some symptoms, don't get at the cause of the problem.

The gas that isn't caused by swallowed air is the natural by-product of the breakdown of foods in the gastrointestinal tract. The ordinary gut holds about three ounces of gas, disposing of it inconspicuously by absorption into the bloodstream. The problem arises when the foods we eat produce too much gas. Foods rich in complex carbohydrates like beans, bran, broccoli and cabbage tend to be the biggest gas producers. Other common offenders: raisins, bananas, popcorn, onions, peanuts, coffee and chocolate. Ironically, spicy foods don't cause much gas, but bland milk does.

Contrary to advertising jingles, everybody does *not* need milk. In fact, some bodies—particularly those approaching their middle years—can't tolerate the stuff. For some reason, production of lactase (the enzyme needed to digest milk sugar) slows in many people as they age. By 40, almost all Asians lack the enzyme and thus find milk indigestible. Anywhere from 30 to 70 percent of blacks, Hispanics, American Indians and dark-skinned whites eventually become milk-intolerant, while almost 10 percent of light-skinned whites are affected. Gas is a major symptom of milk intolerance. If you are so afflicted, you will either want to omit those dairy products causing problems (yogurt, cheddar and cottage cheese are often okay) or add a lactase product (Lact-Aid is sold in pharmacies) to your milk.

IRRITABLE BOWEL SYNDROME (IBS)

If you get stomach cramps when you're nervous or endure alternating bouts of constipation and diarrhea during times of stress, you're one of 22 million Americans who suffer from IBS. This classic postindustrial illness triggered by fast-lane living is second only to the common cold as a persistent cause of discomfort and job absenteeism. Those most at risk are bright, well-educated people who pride themselves on being superb organizers and high-level achievers. Experts say two out of three IBS sufferers are women, and most are between the ages of 20 and 45.

Variously referred to as nervous stomach, irritable colon or spastic colon, IBS is a catchall for a variety of functional bowel disorders. It's what you have if the doctor can't find anything physically amiss (an infection, ulcer or tumor, for example), but your colon doesn't behave normally. Instead of pushing food through with regular wave-like movements, the colon contracts with random spasms, moving food erratically though the system. Pain, cramping, constipation and diarrhea are the result.

The problem is often triggered by emotional stress, internalized anger—which is why some experts say women are more IBS-prone than men—and harried life-styles, but doctors also believe diet can play a significant role. The incidence of IBS in the United States seems to parallel our greater consumption of refined sugar, points out physician and author Isadore Rosenfeld. The disorder is most frequently seen in countries where the diet is similar to our own, he says. Furthermore, IBS is often alleviated by dietary changes, regardless of personality type and life-style.

Other experts point an accusing finger at milk products. One Johns Hopkins University researcher estimates that as many as 70 percent of IBS sufferers are lactose-intolerant and don't know it. A recent study at Cambridge University in England found that wheat, corn, coffee, tea and citrus fruits may cause attacks. Doctors believe that beans, broccoli, cabbage, cauliflower and other common gas-producers may also be culprits. Drugs too may aggravate IBS. Caffeine, alcohol, adrenaline and codeine have all been implicated.

What should you do if you experience IBS symptoms?

- Get a checkup. You need to know if you suffer from IBS or some organic disorder requiring particular treatment.
- Cut back on milk products. If symptoms subside, lactose was the villain.
- Eliminate common gas-producing vegetables.
- Omit candy, pastries and other foods loaded with refined sugars.
- Add fiber to your diet, including bran, whole grains and fresh fruits.
- Increase fluids.
- Avoid laxatives. They will only aggravate an already irritable bowel.
- Exercise regularly to reduce tension.

HEARTBURN

Heartburn has nothing to do with the heart—although its intense chest pain may scare you into thinking you're having a heart attack. And, contrary to general belief, it's not a stomach disorder. It's actually an inflammation of the esophagus caused when stomach acid backs up through the muscular valve between the stomach and esophagus. Unlike the stomach, the esophagus has no mucous lining to protect it from gastric acids.

Normally, the valve opens to allow food into the stomach while keeping stomach contents from flowing back up and acting on the bare walls of the esophagus. But a number of things can cause the system to go awry. Overeating can cause abdominal pressure to relax the valve. Certain foods like chocolate, fats, oils, mints and carbonated beverages can also lessen the tension of the valve. Nicotine and alcohol have similar effects. Hearty partying, which may combine several overindulgences, is thus a prime cause of heartburn.

Air swallowers may also experience heartburn when their bloated stomach increases pressure on the esophageal valve. So may pregnant women when an expanding uterus pushes against the stomach and releases the valve. Life-style may be a factor too. Stress and tension stimulate the flow of gastric juices. Eating on the run or eating while working often means poorly chewed food, an overworked stomach and increased abdominal pressure.

The fastest cure for heartburn is a few swallows of water or food—anything that washes away the irritating acid in the esophagus. Antacids may also provide relief by neutralizing stomach juices. But the only permanent cure comes from changing eating and life-style habits.

CONSTIPATION

We tend to think of constipation as an inevitable consequence of growing older. It isn't. It's true that an aging colon loses some muscle tone. It's also true that the wave-like contractions in the colon—the motion that pushes waste through the system—grow a bit sluggish. But the colon, like the rest of the digestive tract, was designed to function adequately even when not operating at peak performance. The problem, say doctors, is really not the colon. It's the poor nutrition, lack of exercise and laxative abuse.

What happens when we're constipated is that the indigestible or slow-to-digest material reaching the colon stays there too long. The longer it remains, the more moisture is absorbed, making it dense, hard and difficult to eliminate. Doctors used to think constipation was a harmless, although perhaps uncomfortable condition. Now new research suggests that years of constipation may contribute to colon or rectal cancer. The longer the material is in the colon, the longer carcinogens linger in the body, experts say.

Lack of bulk in the diet is the major villain. Our highly processed food just doesn't provide the roughage we need to keep things moving through our lower gut. We may get away with breakfast pastries and gourmet TV dinners in our 20s or even 30s, but once our colon becomes a bit sluggish with age, we need whole grains and fresh fruits and vegetables to stay regular. Not enough fluids can also cause constipation. Inactivity may play a part. So may medications often associated with middle age: tranquilizers, antidepressants and antihypertensives.

Our first reaction to constipation is to run to the drugstore for a laxative. Wrong. Laxatives may actually cause constipation rather than remedy it. (At best, they temporarily solve a problem that demands a long-term cure.) Instead, our first reaction should be to increase fiber in our diet. There's widespread agreement among doctors and researchers that dietary fiber (especially bran) is a safe and effective way of guarding

THE TRUTH ABOUT LAXATIVES

More than 41 million Americans spend in excess of $400 million a year on laxatives. We're not only wasting our money, say most doctors, we may actually be doing ourselves harm.

Those who depend on laxatives are teaching their colons to be lazy. After relying on such products, the colon can "forget" how to function on its own. In other words, frequent laxative use can actually cause constipation.

Doctors suggest adding fiber to the diet and increasing exercise to combat irregularity. If you must take a laxative, they say, use it sparingly and choose a gentle product rather than a stimulant formula. Gentle laxatives work by increasing the bulk in the colon (like Metamucil) or softening stool by causing the colon to retain fluid (like Phillips' Milk of Magnesia). Harsh formulas (castor oil, Carter's Little Liver Pills) work by irritating the lining of the colon so much that the body works hard to get rid of them (and whatever else is in the colon).

against constipation. "No one on a high-fiber diet is going to get constipated," writes Dr. David Rubin in *The Save Your Life Diet*.

Indeed, hundreds of bran-related studies show that it can act as a stool softener, shortening the time it takes for food to pass through the colon. Other research suggests that people who eat high-fiber diets have fewer carcinogen-producing bacteria in their colons than those on low-fiber diets. What should you add to your daily menu? Whole-grain breads and cereals, nuts, raw carrots and other vegetables and fruits, a tablespoon or two of bran.

GALLSTONES

A disease of the overfed or the genetically unlucky, gallstones are hardened masses of cholesterol, blood and bile salts. Sometimes microscopic, sometimes as big as oversized marbles, the stones form in the gallbladder or the bile duct leading from the gallbladder to the small intestines.

Although no one knows exactly why, far more women suffer from gallstones than men. One theory is that those who frequently gain and lose large amounts of weight—as women do during pregnancies—are more susceptible. A massive two-year survey conducted at Oxford University found that gallstones are twice as common in women over 40 as in middle-aged men and that female vegetarians are two-and-a-half times less likely than other women to develop them. Gallstones, noted the British researchers, are more common in overweight than normal-weight women, and the risk increases with age.

Fortunately, as many as 75 percent of those with gallstones experience no symptoms and require no treatment. The stones may float harmlessly in the gallbladder. Small stones may pass uneventfully through the bile duct, into the small intestines and out of the body. But for the 25 percent who do suffer, the symptoms are not pleasant. Gallbladder attacks are notoriously painful and may be accompanied by chills, fever, vomiting and jaundice. Others may suffer long-term abdominal discomfort, indigestion and nausea.

Although gallstones are associated with growing older, once again, age is not the culprit. Good living is. Scientists have found that a high-calorie diet is linked to increasing amounts of cholesterol in the bile and to the formation of gallstones. Total calories—not the cholesterol in the diet (which has little relationship to the cholesterol in bile)—are to blame. Obviously the best hedge against this potentially gut-wrenching problem is a moderate diet that allows you to maintain a normal weight.

For those who do develop gallstones and suffer acute or long-term attacks, doctors usually recommend surgical removal of the gallbladder. A less harrowing but so far less successful treatment makes use of cholesterol-dissolving drugs. A newer, still experimental treatment uses shock waves to pulverize gallstones.

DIVERTICULOSIS

Diet is most probably the culprit in yet another gut problem common in aging digestive systems: diverticulosis. Diverticula are outpouchings of the large intestine, finger-like projections of the colon lining through weak spots in the muscle wall. Some scientists say that the formation of these little pockets is a natural part of the aging process. The muscles of the colon wall weaken with age, they say, making these ruptures more probable. But many researchers vehemently insist that age alone is not the cause.

They point to evidence that diverticulosis is a relatively new condition. In 1930, according to Mayo Clinic records, only 5 percent of patients older than 40 had diverticulosis. The 1980 records showed that more than 30 percent of the same age group were affected. Figures from other sources confirm the increase of diverticulosis from a rare condition to one currently affecting as many as 33 percent of middle-aged Americans. If normal aging were to blame, these statistics would make no sense.

Those who look at the changing dietary habits of our society think they have the answer. Highly refined, processed foods have taken over. From the socially acceptable croissant to the laughable loaf of Wonder bread, Americans are eating less and less fiber. And, say the experts, a consistent, lifelong low-fiber diet is the most likely cause of diverticulosis. What happens, they think, is that the colon must contract more often and more forcefully when its contents are not sufficiently bulky. When this pressure occurs repeatedly over a long period of time, little pockets pop out of the intestinal wall. Bulk in the colon—more fiber—means fewer, more gentle muscular contractions and less chance of ruptures.

Although diverticulosis is common, it is generally symptomless and does not interfere with the digestion. But in 10 to 20 percent of the cases, the outpouchings become inflamed and infected. That's when diverticulosis, the condition, becomes diverticulitis, the disease. Sufferers may endure intense pain and chronic constipation. The treatment? Increased dietary fiber. In severe cases, the inflamed pocket may abscess, perforate and infect the abdominal cavity.

ULCERS

They were once thought to be an "executive ailment," dues extracted from the corporate ladder-climber on the way to a vice-presidency and a posher suburb. But now researchers say there is no evidence that ulcers strike those in any particular occupations or social or financial strata.

It is true that some people—irrespective of career or

bankbook—react strongly to stress by producing excess gastric acid. Over time, this may eat away at the lining of the stomach or duodenum (the first section of the small intestine), causing painful sores known as ulcers. Coffee, alcohol, aspirin and hurried eating habits also increase acid production. Some people may be predisposed to ulcers because of a thinner, less protective gut lining. Another theory suggests that those with type O blood are, for reasons not yet known, more susceptible.

Historically, ulcers have been far more common in men than women, but the rate for both sexes is declining. In the early 1960s, ulcers affected an estimated one in ten men. Today less than one in 20 men and perhaps one in 50 women have ulcers. No one really knows why the numbers have decreased. Some doctors suspect that the widespread use of over-the-counter antacids may help counteract excess acid before it ulcerates the stomach or duodenum lining. Others suggest that everything from running to yoga helps dissipate stress before it turns inward.

But no one credits milk-drinking, once thought to be the great ulcer cure. In fact, studies have shown that protein and calcium actually stimulate the production of stomach acid. The traditional bland diet doesn't help either. More than 30 years of research points to no difference in the healing of ulcers among those on restricted diets and those who ate what they wanted.

HOW TO KEEP YOUR GUT YOUNG

Yes, the digestive tract ages. But the system itself is designed to take aging in stride—if only we don't gum up the works. Here's how to keep the digestive tract functioning well for a lifetime:

- Eat a high-fiber diet. Sufficient bulk in the colon keeps the system working smoothly. Lack of dietary fiber is linked to constipation, diverticulosis and other bowel problems. High-fiber foods include: bran, whole grain breads and cereals, fresh fruits and vegetables.
- Eliminate foods that cause you digestive distress. Some people may have problems with gas-producing vegetables like broccoli, cauliflower and cabbage. Others may find milk products less and less digestible. If you suffer cramps, gas, diarrhea or constipation, think back to what you ate during the past 48 hours.

BE KIND TO YOUR GUT

Digestive distress shouldn't send you running to the medicine cabinet for, at best, temporary relief. Instead, it should signal you that it's time to take inventory of your eating and drinking habits. Many common foods, beverages and medications have been linked to gut problems. Cutting out the offending substances often permanently cures the problem.

If you experience:	Cut back on these common offenders:
Heartburn	coffee, chocolate, alcohol, onions, peppermint
Stomach pain	coffee and caffeine drinks, alcohol, nicotine, aspirin, arthritis medication, asthma medication, antihypertensives, antibiotics
Gas, bloating, bowel distress, diarrhea	milk and milk products, saccarin-sweetened products, coffee, tea, peanuts, broccoli, cabbage, beans, garlic
Constipation	white bread, pastries and other highly processed, refined foods; antidepressants, antihistamines, diuretics

- Moderate calories. Overeating can cause stomach bloat, heartburn and bowel distress. High-calorie diets have been linked to gallstones.
- Practice good eating habits. Make mealtime relaxing. Don't eat on the run, eat while talking or gulp hot liquids. Following these

commonsense habits can save you from indigestion, heartburn and even ulcers.

- Reduce or eliminate alcohol, caffeine and nicotine. These common—and commonly abused—drugs are stomach and bowel irritants that may cause heartburn and indigestion as well as worsen ulcers or IBS.
- Be an aware drug consumer. Some medications are not kind to the digestive tract. Aspirin, antihistamines, diuretics, antihypertensives, sedatives and other substances can cause distress. Ask your doctor about potential side effects of all medications.
- Don't overuse laxatives, antacids or other over-the-counter remedies. At best, they relieve only symptoms. At worst, they encourage the digestive tract to become dependent on something other than its own processes.
- Reduce daily stress or develop ways of coping with it. Burying tension and internalizing anger are two good ways to wreak havoc on the digestive system.
- Exercise regularly. It helps to control weight, reduce stress and keep the bowel functioning normally.

16

Fighting Disease

The world is not a friendly place. Anyone who thinks it is should remember the "Boy in the Bubble," who lived his life in a plastic-lined, germ-free environment, breathing filtered air. An unprotected walk in the woods could have meant death. A kiss could have been fatal.

The Boy in the Bubble suffered from a condition that robbed him of an immune system. Without it, he was defenseless. And to the defenseless, the world is a killer.

Luckily, his condition is rare. Most of us safely traipse through swarms of potential assassins — bacteria, fungus, parasites — unconscious of the hundreds of tiny wars our bodies fight every day to rid us of the invaders. Fighting these battles for us is a carefully balanced army of one thousand billion white blood cells, controlled through a complex relay of chemical signals sent by the cells themselves, associated glands and the nervous system. This immune army protects us from disease—and may lie at the heart of the aging process.

The immune system is certainly a key factor in aging. It is one of the first bodily systems to decline with age, and its loss of protective power is believed to trigger a number of other problems.

- Most cases of the so-called "diseases of aging" — cancer, heart disease, arthritis, and infectious diseases like pneumonia — happen only after the immune system begins showing signs of age. Without its guardian army in top shape, the older body falls prey to ailments it once easily fought off.

- It appears the immune system also helps cleanse the body of dead and defective normal cells. Along with its decline comes a build-up of cellular garbage that may contribute to the aging of other organs.
- The aging immune system often begins attacking the body it's supposed to protect.
- Preliminary evidence suggests that the same genes controlling the immune system may also be the timekeepers of the aging process.

FOOT SOLDIERS AND OFFICERS

During the past few decades, scientists have been increasingly interested in the functioning of the immune system and the causes of its decline. Unfortunately, it's not an easy system to understand. Only recently have researchers begun to unravel the complex interplay of cells, glands and chemical messengers that help the immune army function—and there is still much to learn.

The soldiers themselves, the white blood cells, fall into two major groups. The first, called phagocytes, are scavengers that indiscriminately engulf and eat foreign invaders.

The second and more important group, called lymphocytes, are able to recognize and respond to individual enemies. Lymphocytes come in two broad types: T-cells and B-cells. Each has its own way of protecting the body, and each is necessary for the full functioning of the other.

B-cells are the foot soldiers of the immune army. Their main job is to produce chemicals called antibodies that act like weapons fashioned specifically for attacking a single type of invader. When antibodies latch onto their target, they can stimulate a series of other chemical reactions that result in its destruction.

After B-cells have recognized an invader and geared up their antibody production, they have the ability to "remember" that invader should it ever come back. The response the second time is quicker and more effective. That's why, once you get the measles, you're very unlikely to get it again; your body "remembers" the measles virus and fights it off the rest of your life. And that's why vaccinations work. Vaccines contain killed or impotent strains of dangerous viruses or bacteria. This fake attack force is alarming enough to wake up your B-cells and give them that important immune memory, but not enough to give you the disease. Once alerted, the B-cells are ready to fight off the real culprits should they mount an attack.

T-cells, despite the vital role played by their B-cell cousins, are rapidly proving to be the more important of the two lymphocyte types. Like sergeants and lieutenants, they both fight and direct the fighting. Various subgroups of T-cells work together to control the immune army through a complex system of chemical commands. T-cells help stimulate the immune system when danger is imminent and damp down the immune response when it gets too strong.

They do their own fighting from close range. While B-cells work from afar, shooting antibodies at invaders, T-cells require direct contact to recognize and destroy the enemy. They are especially important in destroying cancer cells.

The *thymus*, master gland of the immune system, acts as both officers' training school and command central for T-cells. Immature white blood cells, raw recruits, travel from the bone marrow to the thymus to be turned into mature, functioning T-cells. The thymus also makes hormones that circulate throughout the body and help T- and B-cells interact effectively.

While each component of the immune system is important on its own, no single part can work effectively without the others helping out. The mechanics of that interplay are still somewhat mysterious.

NORMAL AGING

Unfortunately, this vital, delicate system is one of the first to be affected by normal aging. Anatomists recognized the problem more than a century ago. When dissecting corpses of various ages, they noted that the brain shrinks a little with age, the muscles deteriorate a bit and liver size decreases slightly. But the most striking age-related change they saw was in the thymus.

This flat, pink, two-lobed gland nestled under the sternum reaches its full size, about 1 1/2 ounces, around age 11. With the onset of puberty, the thymus starts shrinking rapidly. By age 40, it is only 10 to 15 percent the size it was in childhood.

And that spells trouble for the immune system. It appears that as the thymus deteriorates, it produces fewer of the hormones that help keep T- and B-cells in order. It becomes less effective in changing immature white blood cells into fully functioning T-cells. And as those all-important T-cells are less able to do their job, the whole immune army is thrown out of step. Because the thymus deteriorates early, the immune system's power peaks in adolescence and goes downhill from there.

The problem is one of quality, not quantity. You have about the same number of white blood cells at age 80 as you did at age 20. But the white blood cells no longer mature as they should; they stop sending and receiving commands as effectively. Sometimes they have trouble getting to where they're needed.

As a result, the whole system becomes less effective. T- and B-cells don't work together as well to kill and clear invaders, leaving older people easier prey for infection. Rates of tuberculosis, influenza, pneumonia, tetanus and other infectious diseases go up.

Higher rates of cancer in older people also reflect an immune system gone awry. Researchers hypothesize that cancer cells crop up in our bodies at roughly the same rate throughout life. But while younger immune systems, particularly T-cells, effectively locate and kill malignant cells before they can multiply and cause trouble, there's more chance that the older immune system will miss the danger.

While most of the system grows weaker, one undesirable type of antibody response gets stronger with age: an *autoimmune* response that turns your defense system against your own body.

It happens when your immune system starts making mistakes in identification, acting as though your own cells are the enemy. B-cells start producing autoantibodies targeted to your nerves, the lining of your blood vessels or other normal cells. Autoantibodies can be found in the blood of nearly every older American, and researchers suspect they play a part in conditions ranging from heart disease and arthritis to neurological ailments.

What makes B-cells start producing these self-destructive chemicals? Researchers believe the answer lies not in the B-cells themselves, but in their regulators, the T-cells. It appears that the sub-group of T-cells responsible for damping down an overactive immune response are especially hard-hit by aging. As their control loosens, the theory goes, B-cells are freed to produce increasing amounts of antibodies to the self.

Autoantibodies, when well regulated, may play a helpful role in ridding the body of damaged tissue. But two pieces of evidence point to them as one of the root causes of aging itself.

In one experiment, researchers injected T- and B-cells from one mouse into another. The added immune cells recognized their new host as an enemy, and began attacking many of its normal cells. The scientists found that the host mice began looking and behaving as though they were quickly aging.

Second, researchers have found that people with higher concentrations of autoantibodies in their blood tend to run increased risks of cancer and heart disease, and have generally shorter life spans.

A shrinking thymus, out-of-whack T- and B-cells and elevated levels of autoantibodies add up to problems in the immune system that worsen with age. But, despite an overall lessening of effectiveness, in most ways the immune system continues serving you well throughout life. The phagocytes, those nondiscriminatory enemy-eaters, don't appear to lose any of their power with age. Although your ability to fight off a *new* infection declines with age, your immune memory response remains unimpaired throughout life. That allows your body to continue to fight off most infections, especially those you've been exposed to before.

As a result, middle age doesn't mean a great increase in infections or cancer. It's not until the immune system goes even farther downhill, in old age, that the "diseases of aging" begin their life-shortening work.

THE CAUSES OF IMMUNE DECLINE

A number of things can knock your immune system off balance, including certain drugs, malnutrition and disease. But for most of us, the key to immune decline appears to lie in the immune system itself. In beginning to sort out the many types of immune cells and the many chemicals they produce to communicate with each other, researchers have begun to trace back defects in the system.

Take autoantibodies as a starting point. Researchers know that autoantibodies are produced in increasing numbers by B-cells, the next step back. Why are B-cells making more? Because they've lost some of the control normally enforced by T-cells. What's wrong with T-cells? The shrunken thymus is not training them efficiently. And why does the thymus shrivel?

No one knows. How cells and organs age is still a mystery (see Chapter 2). Some researchers are looking at the pituitary gland in the brain, long suspected of controlling the timing of aging, which may produce a hormone that interferes with the thymus' work.

Another group is focusing on a group of genes that control much of the immune response. This relatively small set of genes regulates much of the immune system and codes for the factors that tell your immune system what is "self" and what is not.

And at least one set of experiments indicates that this same set of genes may control aging itself. Researchers have bred strains of mice that are genetically identical except for this one set of genes. Even a small change in this set, they have found, can mean up to a 20% increase in lifespan.

Work on this important gene system is still in its infancy and promises to tell us much more about the immune system and aging as it progresses. While it's doubtful that any one master gene for aging is going to be found—if there were such a gene, certainly someone would have been born with a mutation in it and lived to be 200!—it's certain that aging and the immune system are closely linked.

A HEALTHIER IMMUNE SYSTEM

Realizing the importance of the immune system, researchers have been looking for ways to make it stronger. There is no magic cure yet, but much has been learned about the effects of everything from diet to drugs, from tissue implants to the power of positive thinking.

Diet

"You can't be too thin . . ." the saying goes. While it may not apply to every health concern, there is some preliminary evidence that it may be true for the immune system. Take Roy Walford's skinny mice. Walford, a UCLA immunologist, found more than a decade ago that he could grow mice with dramatically "younger" immune systems and longer life spans simply by restricting their diet from very early in life. The trick was providing the animals with enough vitamins and minerals to remain healthy, while slashing overall calories. The result is what Walford calls "undernutrition," as opposed to "malnutrition."

Other studies indicate that a high-fat, low-fiber diet in mice is associated with an increase in autoantibodies, while these self-destructive chemicals are less of a problem for mice on low-fat diets.

Most undernutrition studies on lab animals have shown that it's important to start early in life. Since such studies would be difficult, not to mention unethical, to perform on children, not much has been learned about the effects of this type of regimen on humans—and that lack of human data has kept the question of undernutrition's effects on the immune system controversial. Few if any physicians are ready to recommend undernutrition—and in any case, the idea of starving yourself for longevity isn't appealing to most people.

Adequate amounts of certain minerals and other dietary factors are also important to a healthy immune system.

IMMUNITY BUILDERS

While there's no magic pill that will boost your immunity by itself, adequate amounts of the following nutrients are important for top immune system functioning:

- *Zinc* is important in keeping the whole system, especially the thymus, healthy. Researchers have found that zinc can reverse the depressed immune system of malnourished children and is helpful in bringing new life to the white blood cells of at least some elderly people. Physicians recommend a daily intake of about 15 mg. The average diet provides about 8 or 9 mg. per day. But be careful not to oversupplement: Amounts in excess of 100 mg. per day may actually impair immune functioning.
- *Iron* deficiency can lead to depressed T-cell function, although it seems to have little effect on B-cells.
- *Selenium*, an essential trace mineral, is needed in small amounts to keep phagocytic cells healthy, and has been shown in some experiments to boost overall immunity in lab animals. Be careful: It's easy to overdose on selenium. Take no more than 100 to 200 *micro*grams per day without talking to your doctor.
- *Arginine*, an amino acid, ups the body's production of growth hormone, which in turn stimulates the thymus. Early studies indicate that it helps the immune system—but more work needs to be done in humans.
- *Vitamin C*, in addition to all the other good things it seems to do, also appears to aid the immune system.

Researchers believe it stimulates bacteria-eating phagocytes, may be needed to help thymic hormones work effectively, and in large doses it may help preserve cells from age-related damage by acting as an antioxidant (see Chapter 2 under "Free Radicals").

- *Vitamins E, A, B6* and *pantothenic acid* all have been linked to healthy immune functioning, and a deficiency of any one can depress immunity. But beware of megadoses: Each (except possibly pantothenic acid) is toxic in high amounts.

Temperature

Lowering the body temperature of some experimental animals, especially cold-blooded ones, also seems to rejuvenate the immune system. But this again is an unappealing area for future research. No one seems excited by the thought of chilling out to fight disease.

Immune Stimulants

As more is learned about the immune system, the chances increase of finding natural or synthetic substances that can stimulate it when it begins to decline.

One approach is adding back chemicals or cells the body produces less of as we age. Experiments that have had some success in the laboratory include injecting immune cells or implanting young thymus tissue from young animals into older animals. The problem is that cells from different individuals are recognized as foreign invaders, triggering an immune reaction against them. The steps necessary to lessen that immune response are unpleasant enough at present to make the idea of transplanting some young person's gland or white blood cells undesirable—although similar techniques are used in some extreme cases of disease.

An alternative is to stockpile your own youthful cells for reuse when you're old. At least one group of researchers is looking at the feasibility of collecting and freezing your cells and tissue while you're young for later use. Whether or not this will work won't be known for years.

Experiments with one of the immune system's own hormones are more encouraging. Injections of the thymus-produced hormone thymosin have been shown to improve immune function and lengthen life span in mice. Thymosin's ability to boost the human immune system is also being investigated as a possible aid in cancer therapy.

Selenium, amino acids, antioxidants like BHT, and a number of synthetic drugs also have shown some indications of aiding immunity, at least experimentally—but each has drawbacks, most are dangerous in excess, and no one of them appears to be a cure-all.

Because the immune system naturally "turns on" when it senses a foreign substance in the blood, researchers have also tried boosting the system by injecting substances especially good at kicking off an immune response. Although this type of therapy has had limited success, it simply serves to jump-start the immune system—it doesn't fix the engine.

About the only tried and true remedy for upping your immunity, at least to some things, is something you may not have thought about since you were a kid: a dose of vaccine. Vaccinations are not general remedies for aging, but they do confer specific immunity to a handful of diseases that can be fatal in old age. Americans tend to be blasé about vaccinations, assuming that once you're an adult, you don't need them.

Not so, say physicians. Many people in the United States are underprotected, having been either too young to receive vaccines in childhood, or too busy to get their booster shots. In addition, new vaccines have been developed for some diseases more likely to affect adults.

VACCINATIONS AREN'T JUST FOR KIDS

Don't let memories of the swine-flu vaccine fiasco dissuade you: The benefits of adequate vaccination far outweigh the possible dangers. Many "diseases of childhood," including measles and mumps, can be far more serious if contracted by unimmunized adults. Although medical opinions vary on exactly who needs which vaccination when (and recommendations seem to change every year), start by checking your vaccination history against the following list—then ask your physician if you should have a vaccine update:

Vaccine	Who Should Take It
Diphtheria/ Tetanus	All adults who haven't completed a primary series; those who haven't had a booster for 10 years; unimmunized pregnant women.
Influenza	All adults over 65; anyone whose immune system is weakened. Should be given yearly.
Pneumococcal pneumonia	Many physicians now recommend that every adult over fifty receive the vaccine every five years; adults with chronic illness and/or depressed immune systems; elderly and institutionalized patients.
Measles	Unimmunized adults who have never had the disease.
Mumps	Adults, especially men, who haven't had the physician-diagnosed disease or haven't received the live vaccine.
Polio	Unimmunized travelers to areas with risk of wild virus infection; possibly unimmunized caretakers of children receiving live vaccine.
Rubella	Unimmunized adults who lack detectable rubella antibodies in blood tests, especially women of childbearing age.
Hepatitis B	Health-care workers in contact with blood products; male homosexuals; patients requiring frequent blood transfusions; prostitutes; drug addicts; travelers to areas where the disease is endemic.

THE FUTURE

As scientists continue to unravel the intricacies of the immune system, they may eventually discover the factors responsible for its aging, leading to therapies that will stop the process. The new tools of genetic engineering may someday enable us to treat the immune system's problems at their genetic root.

For the moment, however, one new line of research is exploring a different way to fight disease. It has more to do with cogitation than chemistry. And it involves a new approach to the problem: thinking your immune system young.

Researchers have known for years that stress and depression can impair the immune response. The classic example is of a grieving spouse who, after a loved one dies, falls prey to ulcers, a heart attack or infection. Forty years ago one researcher tested the blood of widowers and found that grief temporarily depressed their immune systems.

That observation lay unappreciated until years later, when researchers found that they could train rats to depress their immune systems on cue. Spurred by this new evidence, researchers began looking for more indications of a link between the nervous and immune systems. Although the concept is still controversial, what they've found recently has pointed to the importance of our minds in regulating the immune system.

- The thymus, spleen and other areas where white blood cells are concentrated are all laced with nerves—for no known reason.
- White blood cells have places on their surfaces designed to receive chemicals produced and used by the nervous system.
- These same nervous-system chemicals have been found to play a role in two immune-related diseases: arthritis and asthma.
- If the thymus is removed early in life, the development of both the nervous and hormonal systems is severely affected.
- Damage to certain parts of the brain can impair immune function.
- Many types of stress, even as minor as that undergone when taking a final exam, can lower the immune system's effectiveness.

Although this new way of looking at immune function has yet to be experimentally proven—and many scientists are skeptical of the whole idea—these discoveries may lead to a revolution in our understanding of and control over the immune system. A few physicians have already begun putting these early findings to use in helping to slow the immune decline and maximize health.

Some of their early findings are encouraging:

- The effect of stress on the immune system appears to depend on how much control the subjects feel they have over their situation. Feelings of helplessness, depression and anxiety worsen the immune-system decline.
- Relaxation techniques designed to ease stress—consciously tightening and loosening muscle groups, for instance—also appear capable of boosting the immune response.
- Researchers are taking a new look at the effects of placebos—inactive substances that sometimes result in miraculous cures if the patient *believes* they're effective.
- Physicians are testing the effects of "hope-enhancing exercises" and visualization techniques, as well as behavior and attitude, on patients with severe disease.

This new research into what one scientist calls the "exquisite relationship" between the conscious mind, the physical brain and the immune and hormonal systems may help us slow the decline of the immune system the easiest possible way: thinking good thoughts.

17
Sex and Hormones

George Edouard Brown-Séquárd thought he had found the fountain of youth. In 1882, this venerable, 72-year-old scientist injected himself with a watery extract from the testes of young dogs and guinea pigs. The results, he wrote, were wonderful: He felt young again, rejuvenated.

Thus began a century-long scientific love affair with the relationship of hormones, sex and aging. Brown-Séquárd's work was a natural outgrowth of the observations that as women age, they undergo a definite change in their hormonal system called menopause. As men age, their sex drive seems to diminish. Researchers at the turn of the century thought that hormones—especially sex hormones—held the key that would unlock the secrets of aging. To this day, quack "clinics" around the world still rake in millions of dollars by offering hormone therapy to bring back lost youth.

But we now know that Brown Séquárd's rejuvenation was more in his mind than the rest of his body. Our hormonal system, while important in normal aging, doesn't appear to run the show by itself. But it *is* important in very visible signs of aging, including menopause and changes in sexual drive.

THE ENDOCRINE SYSTEM

The body has two great controlling systems. One is electrical—the nervous system. The other is chemical—the endocrine system. The endocrine system is comprised of a set of glands that produce hormones, chemicals that carry messages to various parts of the body.

Both systems help keep the body in internal balance. The endocrine system does this by sensing small changes in body chemistry and reacting to bring them back to normal.

THE BODY'S BALANCING ACT

In order to function properly, the body has to maintain a fine and constant balance—something scientists call *homeostasis*. That means body temperature has to be kept within a few degrees of normal. Blood chemistry has to be equilibrated. Heartbeat must increase and decrease in response to stress. This delicate balancing act helps determine our health throughout life.

Your body accomplishes it through feedback systems that work something like the thermostat in your home. When a thermometer in the thermostat senses a low temperature, it sends a signal to the furnace to turn on the heat. More heat raises the temperature, turns off the thermometer's signal to the furnace, and the furnace rests.

With the endocrine system, the feedback signals are nerve impulses or minute changes in the levels of the chemicals in the body. Sensing these changes, the glands secrete small amounts of hormones that act to maintain the balance. Reflecting this give-and-take, most hormones are secreted cyclically, with a rhythm that can vary from a spurt every few minutes to a monthly cycle—as with menstruation.

The endocrine system works with the nervous system to fine-tune the body's everyday activities, as well as regulate long-term processes such as growth and sexual development.

Connecting the two great controlling systems is a sort of electrochemical switchboard called the *hypothalamus*. This special subsection of the brain is connected via a slender stalk to the tiny *pituitary gland*, a chemical factory as big of the tip as your little finger. The pituitary, often called the master gland of the body, produces eight different hormones.

The hypothalamus and pituitary work together through a complex system of hormone messengers. When the brain senses stress or injury, for instance, the hypothalamus releases chemicals that tell the pituitary to release hormones designed to alter body metabolism, ease pain and give a burst of adrenalin.

By secreting only one millionth of a gram of hormones a day, the pituitary manages to control body size, through a chemical called human growth hormone; sexual development, through two hormones that switch the sex glands on; the rate at which our bodies burn oxygen, through a hormone that stimulates the thyroid gland; our response to stress; even milk production in women after childbirth.

THE ENDOCRINE SYSTEM

Gland	Major hormones produced	Activity
Pituitary	HGH	body growth
	TSH	controls thyroid gland
	ACTH	controls adrenal gland
	FSH and LH	control sex glands
	PL	milk production
	ADH	urine production
	oxytocin	labor contractions
Ovaries	estrogen, progesterone and inhibin	sexual characteristics, pregnancy, menstruation
Testes	testosterone	sexual characteristics
Thymus	thymosins	control immune system
Thyroid	thyroxine calcitonin	metabolism bone formation

Gland	Major hormones produced	Activity
Parathyroid	PTH	calcium/phosphate levels
Adrenal cortex	cortisol aldosterone	stress response, metabolism sodium/potassium balance
Adrenal medulla	epinephrine (adrenaline) and norepinephrine	stress reactions
Pineal	melatonin serotonin	menstrual cycle brain function
Pancreas	insulin and glucagon	control blood sugar

Other tissues that also release hormones and are sometimes considered endocrine glands include the placenta during pregnancy, the kidneys, liver, heart, gastrointestinal tract and lungs.

NORMAL AGING

Given the precision and balance needed to make it all work, it would seem simple for the aging process to upset the endocrine system's functioning, with concurrent health problems.

But the feedback machinery of the endocrine system has built-in safeguards to insure that doesn't happen. The aging thyroid gland, for instance, puts a little less of its metabolism-regulating hormone into the blood system as we age—but the older body compensates by breaking down the hormone more slowly, so overall levels stay the same.

In some cases, a slowing in timing of hormone release, a winding-down of the cycles, may also occur with age. But again, the changes that have been found in most cases are balanced by making more of the hormones involved or breaking down less of them, leaving blood levels about the same.

In general, although researchers stress that much more work needs to be done, it appears that normal aging has no great effect on the endocrine system—with three major exceptions:

- The thymus undergoes significant changes with aging that may affect immune functioning (see Chapter 16).
- There is a chance that diabetes will develop in some older people, a problem linked to hormonal change.
- Changes in the ovaries lead to menopause and related problems.

AGE-RELATED DIABETES

The body's ability to keep blood sugar in balance depends on insulin, a hormone produced by the pancreas. Insulin tells cells in the liver and the rest of the body to take in glucose.

If enough insulin isn't produced, sugar builds up in the blood and causes a number of problems. This is Type I or insulin-dependent diabetes. Its effects are usually seen in childhood and can be treated with insulin shots. If untreated, it can lead to death.

Type II diabetes, also called "maturity onset" or insulin-independent diabetes, accounts for 90 percent of all cases. It affects mostly adults older than age 40. Even though adults generally start producing less insulin in their 30s and continue the decline through old age, researchers don't think that an insulin shortage is the problem with Type II diabetes. Instead it appears that the insulin that is produced doesn't have as much effect on the body's cells.

Hereditary factors play an important role. But part of the problem, investigators think, is also related to the fact that muscle takes up more sugar than does fat. Because aging usually means a decrease in lean muscle and a build-up of fat, some older bodies are less able to effectively regulate blood-sugar levels. Obese people run a greater risk of Type II diabetes.

National Institute on Aging researchers who studied Type II diabetes have recommended increased exercise to keep the proportion of muscle to fat high. Changes in diet have also successfully treated the condition.

Gestational diabetes is a transient condition that can affect pregnant women, especially those older than 35 who have a family history of the disease. It is treated through dietary changes and generally disappears after childbirth.

HORMONES AND SEX

At a recent national meeting of the American Association for Retired People, the runaway hit among all the seminars offered was titled "Sex after 60." Such strong interest should help puncture the myth that old people are not sexually active. Biologically, there is no reason to expect a decrease in sexual satisfaction as we age. And for many people, sex at an older age means more experienced, more comfortable, less inhibited, *better* sex.

The primary hormones that direct sexual development are *testosterone*, produced by the testes (and to a small degree the adrenal glands) in men, and *estrogen* made in the ovaries (and a bit in the adrenals) in women. These two sex hormones start making us what we are—male or female—in the womb.

It appears that the basic structural plan for mammals, including humans, is female—until told to be otherwise. What does the telling in men is testosterone, and the directions begin before birth. Both men and women produce female and male sex hormones, but in men testosterone predominates; in women, estrogen.

The sex hormones may do much more than determine the model of reproductive apparatus we are equipped with. In recent years, a great deal of excitement has centered on the discoveries that men's and women's brains are structurally different and that sex hormones can affect the structure of brain cells. These findings have led some researchers to the hypothesis that male/female mental differences may be hormonally set. While it is still far too early to pin down hormonal effects on behavior, some enthusiasts are already postulating a sex-related biological basis for everything from math skills and homosexuality to verbal ability and criminal tendencies. Looking for the roots of such behavioral and mental effects "in the blood" has been a favorite pastime of bigots and social engineers for centuries. Until this hot scientific controversy cools down, it is best not to ascribe too much power to hormones.

Sex hormones are produced at a low rate through childhood, and then shoot up to adult levels during a few years in adolescence, triggering the changes called puberty.

WOMEN AND SEXUAL CHANGE

Changing Hormones

For women, puberty begins when the ovaries mature and begin releasing sex hormones in response to commands from the pituitary. A feedback system is started: The pituitary releases hormones to tell the ovaries to make estrogen and progesterone; high levels of these hormones in the blood are detected by the brain and pituitary, which in turn stop making the triggering hormones.

As all these hormones reach adult levels, menstruation begins, breasts grow and changes in fat and muscle begin shaping the female body.

In their early to mid-40s, most women's ovaries begin making less and less estrogen. The final stage of this process, menopause, happens when the ovaries stop responding to commands from the pituitary to make estrogen. Some estrogen is still made by the adrenal glands and in peripheral tissues—about 20 percent of the levels found before menopause—but it's not enough to maintain menstruation. The cycle stops.

The result, at least temporarily, is a body in hormonal turmoil. As the blood level of estrogen drops, the pituitary tries to compensate by making more of the hormones that tell the ovaries to make estrogen. This increase can kick off "hot flashes"—intense feelings of heat over the face and perspiration on the chest—and night sweats in some women. These symptoms vary in intensity from case to case; many women don't experience them at all. The brain tries to compensate for this increase by lowering its production of the hormone that tells the pituitary to make the runaway estrogen-triggering hormones.

And the loss of estrogen by itself has effects. The most common are a shrinking and drying of the vagina and a thinning of the urethral wall. That leads to an increased chance of inflammation in the area and occasional difficulty in urination. Estrogen loss may also signal a time of increased bone loss in susceptible women (see Chapter 10).

Complicating a woman's response to these changes is the often discussed "postmenopausal depression." Whether changing hormonal levels play a role in this condition is unclear. What is known is that this period of life is difficult for many other reasons: The end of menstruation is a sign that old age is approaching, children commonly leave home, career and family situations may change.

The important point is that attitudes and experiences among postmenopausal women vary greatly. Depression and discomfort aren't inevitable. There is no preset syndrome that every woman goes through and no predetermined roster of symptoms to dread.

In severe cases of menopausal discomfort, physicians sometimes prescribe estrogen-replacement therapy. It appears valuable in relieving some physical symptoms, but it has its risks (see Chapter 10 for the pros and cons of estrogen therapy). It is also prescribed occasionally for postmenopausal depression—but watch out. Unless the depression is caused by physical discomfort, there is no guarantee that estrogen therapy will help. If depression becomes a problem at any stage of life, seek counseling.

The Effect on Sex

At least in the realm of sex, women appear to age better than men. Age-related hormonal changes in women do not result in any important alterations in their arousal time or ability to have orgasms. Men (see below) are not quite so lucky.

That is not to say that menopause won't have any effect at all. Drying of the vagina may lead to some discomfort during intercourse. Changes in lubrication can be overcome by taking longer with foreplay and using lubricants. Exercising muscles in the pelvic region may help counter the looseness that can result from vaginal shrinking.

SEX AND EXERCISE

In 1952, gynecologist Arnold Kegel found that a set of pelvic exercises he developed to help incontinent women retain their urine had a pleasant side-effect: Some of his patients were having orgasms for the first time.

His exercises, now called "Kegels," are still used for treating incontinence and aiding childbirth. But they also serve to strengthen muscles that squeeze and tighten the vagina. Keeping them toned can help increase pleasure in sex at any age, but especially after menopause.

Kegels are easy to learn. Because the muscles involved are the same that stop urination, you can identify them by trying to stop your flow while urinating. Keep your legs spread apart so that your buttock muscles won't interfere. You may not be able to completely stop the flow the first time, but you should be able to feel the muscles involved. They are also tightening your vagina. By the time you're able to stop and start your flow three times, you'll have it.

Clenching this muscle several times a day will help tone and train it. But don't stop there. A well-exercised body provides a better self-image and increased energy that can help sexual feelings and performance, so be sure to keep in overall shape.

And remember that the best exercise for sex is—sex. Researchers have found that sexual performance and pleasure get better for most people the more often they partake.

But the biggest obstacle to sex for older women is older men. There just aren't enough of them to go around. In the 65-and-older age group, women outnumber men three to two, and men are twice as likely to be married. Sexual satisfaction seems to depend on how often you have sex—the more often the better—so a lack of partners can be a major problem.

MEN AND SEXUAL CHANGE

Compared with dramatic age-related changes in a woman's hormonal state, men are sticks-in-the-mud. Although testosterone levels do decrease a small amount with age in some men, the decline is slow and steady rather than sudden, so there are no resulting dramatic physiological effects. There is some effect on the timing of hormonal release: Young men's testosterone levels peak in the morning, while older men's stay at the same level all day.

While some researchers blame this slight drop in testosterone for everything from a loss of muscle to a weakened libido, most now believe that it has little if any effect on sexual function or anything else. The ability to father children, for instance, doesn't decline until very old age—and some men have become fathers in their 90s. Sperm function and semen volume stay close to normal at all ages. Supplemental

THE PROSTATE PROBLEM

The male prostate gland, located at the bladder outlet, normally functions to provide fluid for semen. But sometimes it seems the prostate's real purpose is to give men trouble.

Normally the size of a walnut, most men's prostates begin ballooning in later life. In some cases, this enlargement doesn't progress far enough to present a problem. But in 10 percent of men older than 50, it will enlarge enough to interfere with the flow of urine. The solution is surgery to remove the prostate or reduce its size. Total removal can lead to impotence; the more common partial removal, while it may reduce the volume of semen ejaculated, usually has no other effect on sexual pleasure.

---

testosterone injections don't seem to have much effect and can increase the risk of prostate enlargement.

But a number of physical changes do occur that can affect sexual functioning. It takes men longer to get aroused as they age, and it takes longer to reach orgasm. The orgasm itself is briefer and ejaculation less forceful. The penis becomes flaccid faster after an orgasm, and it takes longer to get a second erection.

These things aren't all necessarily bad. More foreplay to establish an erection and a longer period before orgasm may be good news, in particular to female sex partners. But along with this comes a gradual decrease in sex drive. One study found that the average male at age 30 had 121 orgasms per year; by age 70 this dropped to 22 per year. The problem, however, isn't universal. The "most active" group of men older than 60 were still having orgasms at the rate of 94 per year—about twice a week.

Why the decline in activity? The causes are complex and inter-related, including both psychological and physiological factors. Fatigue, tension, illness, drugs, alcohol and simple fear of loss of potency can all play a role. A sedentary life-style can lead to an overall loss of energy and a poor self-image, which can also contribute to a lack of sexual feelings.

It was once thought that 90 percent of all cases of impotence was psychological in origin. But researchers are now finding that many more cases have a physiological basis than was previously thought. Better diagnosis techniques have helped distinguish the two, and new therapies are helping treat a number of men with physical problems.

POTENCY FOREVER

Failure to achieve erection is something that can happen at any age—but for older men, it happens more often. Luckily, medical science is providing ways of dealing with the problem.

Physicians faced with cases of erectile impotence first have to decide if the condition is in the mind or the body. Since most physically healthy men have erections while asleep, a common test consists of wrapping a roll of postage stamps around the penis before bedtime. If morning finds them torn along the perforation, chances are the impotency is psychological in origin. The treatment is counseling.

There are many causes of and treatments for nonpsychological impotence. Recently, two devices have been developed to correct the condition when nothing else works. One is a semirigid rod implanted in the penis that can be adjusted to any angle. Another is an inflatable system that uses a handpump implanted in the scrotum. Both have had great success.

Other research is pointing toward the age of push-button potency. Electrical stimulation of certain nerves in the pelvic area, one research group has found, can cause erections. One chimpanzee fitted with a battery system was able to have erections on demand, regardless of the time since orgasm.

Overall physical fitness is again important. A healthy, well-exercised, disease-free body is not only more desirable to the opposite sex, it is an important factor in maintaining an interest in sex.

But both men and women should remember that the most powerful sexual organ is the brain. Developing and maintaining relaxed, pleasure-filled attitudes toward intercourse may be the most important thing you can do to assure a lifetime of good sex.

INDEX